TRANSFORMATION THAT LANDS

A LEADERSHIP PLAYBOOK FOR THE DIGITAL AGE

SRIDHAR RAVILLA

Acknowledgments

This book reflects the collective experiences of many people and moments, not the work of a single individual.

First, I'm deeply grateful to the teams and colleagues I've worked alongside across geographies and organizations. Many of the insights in this book were shaped in real transformation environments during late-night decisions, difficult trade-offs, and moments when execution either held or collapsed under pressure. The lessons here belong as much to those teams as they do to me.

I'm thankful to the mentors and leaders who challenged my thinking about change, leadership, and accountability. Their willingness to ask uncomfortable questions and demand real answers helped shape the perspective that transformation is not a project, but a leadership capability.

I also want to acknowledge the personal experiences that influenced how I think about transformation beyond systems and strategy. Life events have a way of sharpening perspective, reminding us that change is ultimately human. Those moments reinforced the importance of empathy, resilience, and clarity when leading others through uncertainty.

Finally, my deepest thanks go to my family for their patience, support, and understanding throughout this journey. Their steady presence made it possible to step back, reflect, and turn years of experience into something meant to be shared.

About the Author

Sridhar Ravilla is a senior transformation leader and advisor with over two decades of experience driving large-scale digital, cloud, and AI transformations across global enterprises. He has held senior leadership roles at AT&T and Tech Mahindra, working closely with executive teams and boards to translate transformation ambition into measurable, sustainable business outcomes.

Throughout his career, Sridhar has led complex initiatives spanning legacy modernization, enterprise AI adoption, cloud economics, and operating model redesign. His work focuses on the areas where most transformations struggle — leadership alignment, decision clarity, execution discipline, and value realization. He is known for a practical, operator-driven approach that prioritizes accountability, adoption, and results over theory or hype.

Sridhar is a recipient of the Diversity & Inclusion Champion Award, recognizing his commitment to building high-performing, inclusive teams capable of delivering change at scale. His leadership philosophy reflects a belief that transformation succeeds not through technology alone, but through human judgment, governance, and sustained execution.

He has completed executive education at MIT focused on technology and leadership and holds an MBA from the Jack Welch Management Institute, where he graduated with Welch Honors.

The STRAVIB framework presented in this book was developed through years of hands-on leadership experience and applied research, distilling what actually enables transformations to land and endure.

This book is a work of nonfiction. While real experiences and insights informed the content, some names and identifying details may have been changed to protect privacy.

For permissions, inquiries, or speaking requests, contact:
Ravilla_sridhar@yahoo.com

E-book: 979-8-9944087-2-8

Paperback: 979-8-9944087-1-1

Hardcover: 979-8-9944087-0-4

First Edition, 2025

Table of Contents

Prologue

Why Transformation Feels Harder Than Ever

Let's be honest. Transformation today is more complex, not because leaders have suddenly become less capable, but because the stakes, noise, and expectations have exploded. AI, cloud, data, customer pressure, talent churn everything is moving faster than organizations can absorb.

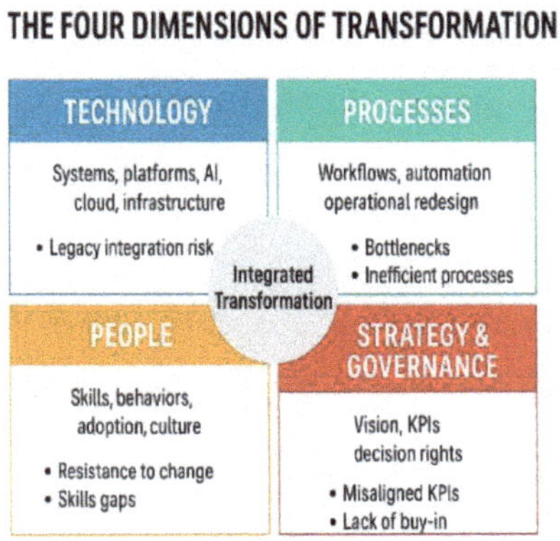

I've watched well-intentioned teams burn time, money, and trust because they were chasing change without a clear map. The gap between strategy decks and real execution has never been wider.

The Promise of This Book

This book is built to close that gap. It's a practical manual for executives, operators, and boards who want transformation that actually sticks. You'll find frameworks you can apply this quarter, not abstract theories. STRAVIB appears as one of the tools, not a silver bullet, but a way to bring clarity, prioritization, and discipline to complex environments. The book centers on one core idea: fundamental transformation is measurable, repeatable, and far less chaotic when leaders clearly understand the game they're playing.

A Personal Turning Point

I didn't learn this from a classroom or a conference. I learned it by leading programs that worked, salvaging those that didn't, and sitting across the table from leaders under real pressure, including missed numbers, shrinking margins, and teams ready to give up. The turning point for me came when I finally stopped treating transformation as a project and started treating it as a capability. Everything shifted after that.

If this book does its job, you'll walk away with the same clarity and a simple thought in the back of your mind: *We could use Sridhar's guidance on this.*

Introduction — The Illusion of Transformation

Transformation is a word that promises more than it usually delivers. Nearly every organization claims it is transforming, yet more than 70 percent of major initiatives fail to achieve their intended outcomes. Some stall halfway. Others burn through budgets with little business impact. A few collapse entirely, leaving behind leadership turnover and no credible way to explain return on investment.

The failure isn't ambition. It's an assumption. Too many leaders equate transformation with activity, such as moving to the cloud, deploying AI, or modernizing legacy systems. Those are inputs, not outcomes. Fundamental transformation is measurable and sustainable, and it is deeply human. It succeeds or fails based on how people make decisions, how accountability is enforced, and how governance supports execution, not on technology alone.

In my twenty years leading global programs at a Tier 1 telecom provider and overseeing transformation portfolios at a GSI, I've seen every type of misstep, from inflated boardroom expectations to grassroots resistance that derails even the most well-funded initiatives. Modern digital and AI transformations amplify both opportunity and risk. The pace of technology adoption and the pressure to deliver tangible results within months, not years, force executives into a trap. They chase outcomes without laying the foundation. They confuse dashboards with progress and meetings with execution.

Transformation has become the corporate equivalent of a participation trophy. Companies use it to describe everything from updating a website to implementing new email software. The word has lost meaning because it is applied to every change initiative, regardless of scope, impact, or business value. When everything is transformation, nothing is transformation.

The $2.7 Trillion AI Transformation Lie

McKinsey says AI will unlock $2.7 trillion. Gartner says most enterprises will be "AI-first." Great headlines. Great consulting proposals. But walk into any Fortune 500 company and ask to see real AI wins. What you'll actually find are half-finished pilots, dusty innovation labs, abandoned proofs of concept, and program charters written two CIOs ago.

The gap between promise and reality is massive.

Harvard Business Review reports that 87% of AI initiatives fail to deliver business value. BCG says 70% of digital transformations miss their targets. These aren't small misses. They are systemic failures that point to something deeper.

Companies pour an average of $15 million into AI transformation and walk away with less than $2 million in measurable value. The math doesn't work, yet the spending continues because nobody wants to admit the truth. We've been chasing a mirage built on hype, fear of missing out, and sales decks promising instant reinvention.

And the lie isn't that AI can't transform a business. It can.

The lie is that transformation requires giant budgets, multi-year epics, and moonshot thinking. In reality, the companies winning with AI are the ones making small, practical moves that compound. Quiet pilots. Focused workflows. Clear ROI. No theater.

Why Transformation Is Overused

Transformation is overused because it sells hope. Consultants, vendors, and even well-meaning executives promote the idea that any system upgrade, AI tool, or digital workflow is transformational. But transformation is not an upgrade. It is a deliberate, repeatable, and measurable shift in business capability. In the real world, transformation requires alignment across strategy, talent, accountability, culture, and execution. Without this alignment, projects become expensive theater.

Consider this. A cloud migration intended to reduce costs may actually triple them if dependencies, integrations, and operational readiness aren't addressed. AI initiatives often fail not because the technology is flawed, but because data is siloed, skills are missing, and expectations are unrealistic. The lesson is simple. Transformation is more than technology. It is leadership under pressure.

Myth vs. Reality

Myth	Reality
Cloud will automatically reduce costs.	Integration, governance, and FinOps matter most.
AI will replace human judgment.	AI augments decisions; adoption requires trust and skill
Modernization is one-time	Continuous investment and hybrid coexistence are essential.

Why Most Transformations Fail

Let's get honest about why transformations fall apart. It's rarely because the technology didn't work. It's because the organization didn't.

There are a few patterns you see over and over.

1. Strategy isn't aligned.
Teams jump into execution without a clear line of sight to what the company is actually trying to achieve. Leaders confuse activity with progress, so everyone stays busy, but nothing moves. When the strategic compass is fuzzy, the entire program drifts.

2. Leaders miss what really slows things down.
Executives often overestimate the speed of change and underestimate the human side. The board dreams in revenue curves while teams are stuck wrestling with data,

legacy systems, and cross-functional turf wars. Optimism bias takes over, and reality never has a chance.

3. Cultural debt drags everything backwards.
Every company has an invisible liability: the habits, norms, and "this is how we do things here" behaviors that quietly resist change and reinforce sunk cost fallacy. You can introduce world-class technology, but if the culture isn't ready, adoption crashes and ROI evaporates.

4. Execution breaks in the middle.
Governance swings between too loose and too bureaucratic. Metrics don't reflect value. Decisions stall. And slowly, the gap between the vision in the boardroom and the reality on the ground widens until the entire effort loses credibility.

Here's what this really means: transformations fail for reasons that have almost nothing to do with the technology itself. They fail because expectations are inflated, incentives don't line up, and execution gets treated like a side project. Leaders think the hard part is declaring the vision. It isn't. The hard part is shifting the everyday behaviors of thousands of people.

Jack Welch called this out in *Winning* years ago. Vision and alignment matter, but poor execution and the wrong expectations will take down even the best strategy. He wasn't talking about cloud or AI, but the lesson fits perfectly. Companies love to celebrate the announcement of a transformation, then act surprised when momentum collapses the moment execution gets messy. And it always gets dirty.

That's the point. Transformation isn't an event. It's a capability. And capabilities require discipline, structure, and a clear-eyed view of how change actually works inside a real business with real constraints.

Modern Digital + AI Context

Digital transformation isn't new, but AI changes the rules. Executives now face pressure to adopt AI rapidly while simultaneously modernizing systems and reimagining business models. AI promises speed, predictive insights, and better decision-making, but without data readiness, aligned teams, and clear ownership, it becomes just another shiny object.

For example, a company I advised had an AI revenue tool that promised to optimize pricing in real time. The board expected results within three months. However, the data was siloed across five systems, and sales teams resisted using the new insights. The initiative struggled, not because AI was incapable, but because leadership underestimated alignment and adoption challenges.

Tool: STRAVIB Early Alignment Table

- Strategy Clarity: Define what success looks like.
- Talent Alignment: Identify critical skills.

- Responsibility Mapping: Assign clear ownership.
- Agility: Set rapid 90-day cycles.
- Value Realization: Define measurable outcomes.
- Integration: Map system dependencies.
- Balance: Ensure innovation doesn't destabilize operations.

Personal Calibration Moments

Stories are not just anecdotes. They are calibration points for decision-making under pressure.

- **Train accident:** Surviving a tragic train accident that claimed 14 lives was a stark reminder of unpredictability. It taught me the importance of anticipating risk, planning for the unforeseen, and remaining composed when reality diverges from expectations. Transformation is no different. Unexpected resistance, technology delays, or talent gaps will arise. Leaders must adapt swiftly and decisively.
- **DEI Champion award:** Recognizing the importance of inclusivity and alignment, this award underscored how human factors drive success. Transformation fails when people are overlooked. Engaging teams, establishing trust, and fostering accountability are as essential as any technology rollout.

What This Book Offers

This book is designed to give you practical, tactical guidance, not academic theory. You'll learn:

- How to run a **transformation that actually lands,** avoiding common pitfalls.
- How to **lead digital and AI initiatives** with clarity and confidence.
- How to **apply a repeatable framework,** STRAVIB®, to every transformation.
- How to **integrate people, technology**, and governance into a cohesive execution plan.

By the end, you'll have a **playbook that boards, executives, and transformation leaders can use immediately,** with practical tools, templates, dashboards, and 90-day cycles that make strategy tangible and measurable.

Chapter Summary:

- Stop confusing activity with progress. Define measurable outcomes.
- Anticipate human resistance and culture debt early.
- Establish strategy clarity and align talent before execution.
- Use STRAVIB to map initiatives, responsibilities, and value.
- Learn from calibration moments. Adapt quickly, trust your judgment, and keep alignment visible.

Transformation is complex, but it is possible. This book is your guide to executing change that delivers results, builds capability, and sets your organization up for the future.

Part I — Understanding the Transformation Landscape

Chapter 1 — The Four Dimensions of Transformation

Transformation isn't one-size-fits-all. Executives often assume that moving systems to the cloud, adopting AI, or updating legacy infrastructure is a single change. The reality is different. Transformation operates across four distinct dimensions, each requiring its own playbook, risks, and measures. Misunderstanding which fight you're in is the fastest way to fail.

FOUR TYPES OF TRANSFORMATION

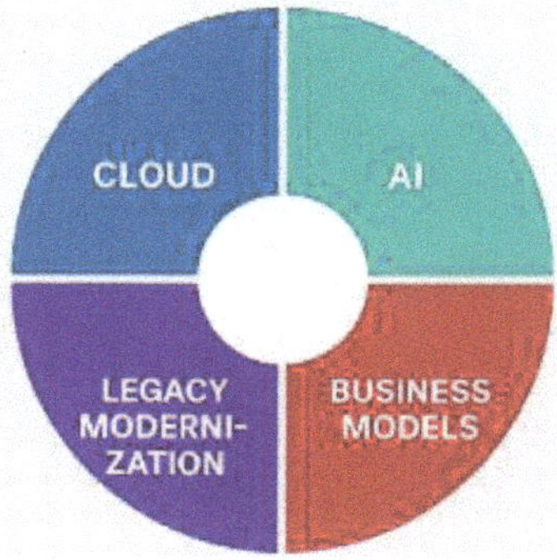

Cloud Transformation

Cloud is often sold as a magic switch, promising lower costs, faster delivery, and instant scale. Anyone who has lived through a real migration knows that promise rarely survives first contact with reality. Moving workloads to the cloud doesn't automatically improve cost, speed, or performance. In many cases, it does the opposite.

The organizations that extract real value from cloud start with a discipline most skip: cost visibility. Cloud spending is dynamic, usage-driven, and far less predictable than traditional IT budgets. Without transparent allocation and real-time reporting, optimization is impossible. Cost control becomes guesswork, and decisions get made in the dark. Mature cost tracking isn't a nice-to-have or a finance exercise. It's the foundation that makes every downstream cloud decision credible.

- **Lift-and-shift vs modernization:** Simply moving workloads without redesigning architecture often leads to cost sprawl and technical debt. True cloud transformation involves modernizing applications, re-architecting for scalability, and continuously optimizing resources.
- **The myth of cost savings:** Organizations frequently see higher operational costs initially due to migration complexity, unexpected dependencies, and governance overhead.
- **FinOps: the CFO's revenge:** Financial oversight often lags behind deployment. Without real-time tracking and accountability, cloud costs balloon faster than leaders anticipate.
- **Case vignette:** A Tier-1 telecom I advised launched a cloud transformation with a simple goal: cut costs by migrating critical enterprise workloads. On paper, it looked like an easy win. In reality, the initial lift-and-shift migrations did the opposite. Hosting costs tripled. Part of the issue was shutting down a home-grown cloud platform too quickly, before teams were ready. The other part was the mismanagement of new cloud instances, which spiraled into significant, unplanned licensing expenses.

Here's the thing: the technology wasn't the problem. Once the systems were in place, agility and integration improved dramatically. But the financial upside only appeared after the company brought discipline to the table, specifically six months of tight FinOps governance, rightsizing, guardrails, and data-driven cost controls. That's when the ROI finally started showing up.

STRAVIB Integration:

- **Strategy Clarity:** Define which workloads truly need cloud modernization.
- **Value Realization:** Measure agility, scalability, and cost efficiency.

AI Transformation

- AI isn't just software. It's a shift in decision-making, not departments. Boards often expect AI to automate everything overnight, while teams struggle with adoption and trust. Decision quality matters more than decision speed for most AI applications. A pricing algorithm that increases margin by 2% while maintaining conversion rates creates more value than one that generates quotes in milliseconds but reduces profitability. Focus on decisions where better accuracy translates into measurable business impact.

- **What AI really transforms:** Decisions, not departments. Human judgment remains central.
- **Hype vs. human:** "AI-first" strategies fail without leadership-first alignment. Teams must understand why AI matters and how it will augment their work.
- **The AI gap:** Many executives have shiny strategy decks, but their data and talent are not ready. Without data pipelines, governance, and ethical guidelines, AI projects falter.
- **Measuring AI ROI:** Go beyond automation savings. Focus on decision accuracy, speed, risk mitigation, and strategic insight.

Case Study: A global digital communications technology firm used AI to modernize a fragmented order-management environment where low flow-through rates and heavy manual intervention were driving cost and delay. Instead of treating AI as a standalone fix, leadership deliberately applied the STRAVIB framework to clarify ownership, align skills, and sequence work into focused 90-day execution cycles.

The outcome was practical rather than theatrical. Flow-through rates increased meaningfully, manual handling was reduced, and order accuracy improved without disrupting day-to-day operations. More importantly, the approach established a repeatable pattern that the organization could apply to automate other high-friction processes while keeping accountability, cost, and adoption firmly under control.

STRAVIB Integration:

- **Talent Alignment:** Identify AI translators—people who bridge data, technology, and business insights.
- **Responsibility Mapping:** Assign ownership for data quality, AI model validation, and adoption.
- **Integration Maturity:** Embed AI into existing workflows rather than replacing them entirely.

Legacy Modernization

The romance of greenfield projects often obscures the pragmatism of brownfield systems. Most organizations cannot afford to start from scratch. Technical debt represents the accumulated cost of shortcuts, workarounds, and compromises made throughout the development and maintenance of a system. Over time, this debt compounds, making systems harder to modify, integrate, and maintain. Technical debt isn't inherently bad, but it requires deliberate and active management.

The hidden cost of technical debt shows up in longer development cycles, more frequent outages, and increasing difficulty integrating with new systems. These costs often exceed the expense of modernization, yet they accumulate gradually in ways that make them difficult to quantify and even harder to address.

- **Technical debt:** Old systems quietly accumulate hidden costs, including maintenance, patching, and workarounds. Ignoring these costs becomes increasingly expensive.
- **Incremental modernization:** Slow, phased updates reduce risk and preserve operational continuity. Big-bang rewrites rarely succeed.
- **Hybrid coexistence:** Legacy and modern systems must coexist during transformation. Careful planning of integration points is critical.
- **Case Study:** A telecom provider attempted to upgrade its order management system in phases. The approach helped prevent major outages, but the real drag came from missing requirements, vendor lock-in, unclear business direction, and messy data. Without a clear responsibility map, teams and suppliers repeatedly worked at cross purposes. The project only stabilized once ownership was clearly defined, requirements were documented, and data cleanup was treated as a first-class workstream.

STRAVIB Integration:

- **Agility in Execution:** Implement 90-day modernization sprints.
- **Value Realization:** Track operational uptime, process efficiency, and customer satisfaction metrics.

Business Model Transformation

Transformation isn't only about technology. It's about how the business creates value. Co-innovation partnerships involve working with customers, suppliers, or even competitors to develop solutions that benefit all parties. These partnerships can accelerate innovation while sharing development costs and risk. Co-innovation works best when partners bring complementary strengths and operate with aligned incentives.

- **Ecosystem plays, partnerships, and co-innovation:** Modern business models often require collaboration beyond the organization.
- **New models:** Subscription, servitization, and platform strategies redefine revenue streams.
- **Why most fail:** Executives misalign incentives, underestimate adoption challenges, or treat business model change as a project rather than a continuous evolution.

Case Study: A software SME pivoted its business from perpetual licenses to a subscription-based model. Early adoption stumbled due to fragmented processes. The company turned it around by realigning incentives, integrating analytics into customer success workflows, and embedding feedback loops to guide both product and process improvements.

STRAVIB Integration:

- **Strategy Clarity:** Align transformation objectives with business model goals.
- **Balance:** Innovate without destabilizing ongoing operations.

Heatmap - Transformation Types vs Readiness: The heatmap serves as a diagnostic anchor, highlighting that different transformations demand different levels of maturity, budget, management rigor, and talent.

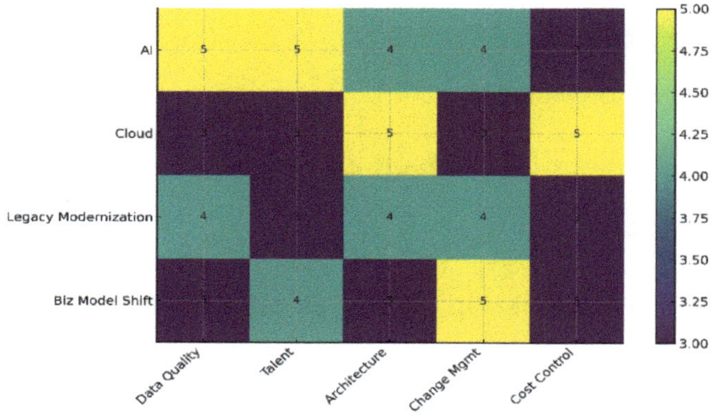

How to read this heatmap

This heatmap compares four transformation types based on complexity, time-to-value, dependencies, and organizational impact. It provides leaders with a quick understanding of what they're facing so they don't treat all transformations the same.

Executive Takeaways

1. **Understand which dimension you're in**—don't apply a one-size-fits-all approach.
2. **Integrate STRAVIB early**— Strategy clarity, talent alignment, responsibility mapping, and value realization are essential.
3. **Phased execution wins**—especially for legacy and cloud modernization.
4. **Measure outcomes, not outputs**—focus on agility, adoption, and strategic impact.
5. **Leadership matters most**—technology is an enabler, not a solution.

Chapter 2 — The Human Side of Change

Transformation is not a technology problem. It is a human problem. Every executive thinks about systems, processes, and data, but the true blockers are human factors such as fatigue, fear, resistance, and culture. Ignoring this side of transformation is the fastest way to stall even the most well-funded initiatives.

Smart executives often fall for transformation scams because consultants tell three lies that sound completely reasonable until examined closely. These lies work because they appeal to executive psychology while obscuring the real complexity that makes transformation difficult. Understanding these lies helps protect leaders from expensive mistakes that damage both careers and budgets.

Lie#1: The first lie is that transformation requires revolutionary thinking and breakthrough innovation. Consultants position transformation as a creative challenge that demands fresh perspectives and outside expertise. They argue that internal teams are too close to existing problems to see truly transformational solutions. This narrative justifies expensive consulting engagements while quietly undermining confidence in internal capabilities.

Lie#2: The second lie is that transformation requires comprehensive change across all business dimensions at the same time. Consultants sell integrated transformation programs that span technology, processes, organization, and culture through tightly coordinated initiatives. They argue that partial transformation creates inconsistencies that undermine overall success. This framing justifies massive project scopes and, in turn, massive consulting fees.

Lie#3: The third lie is that transformation success requires perfect upfront planning and detailed roadmaps that anticipate every challenge and dependency. Consultants produce elaborate project plans with precise timelines, resource assumptions, and milestone definitions. They position exhaustive planning as risk mitigation, claiming it prevents costly surprises during implementation.

Transformation Fatigue

Transformation fatigue is real. Teams are asked to adopt new systems, processes, and mindsets all at once. They attend workshops, complete training modules, and adjust to new KPIs while continuing to fulfill their regular responsibilities.

- **Symptoms:** missed deadlines, passive resistance, decreased quality, or burnout.
- **Impact:** productivity declines, adoption stalls, and ROI evaporate.
- **Executive insight:** leaders often mistake lack of enthusiasm for lack of skill.

STRAVIB Integration:

- **Talent Alignment:** Identify and prioritize “change champions” to carry initiatives forward.
- **Agility:** Use 90-day transformation cycles to pace workloads and reduce fatigue.

Leadership Blind Spots

Even experienced leaders have blind spots that can jeopardize change:

1. **Optimism Bias:** Assuming teams will adapt faster than they can.
2. **Shiny-Object Syndrome:** Chasing the latest tech without considering readiness.
3. **Invisible Sponsorship:** Leaders announce change but don’t actively participate or reinforce it.

Action Tip: Visible leadership is critical. Leaders must show up in workshops, participate in decision-making, and consistently communicate priorities. Leadership absence signals low priority to teams.

Resistance and Culture

Resistance is a natural response to disruption. People fear the unknown, worry about skill gaps, or mistrust motives. Culture amplifies this effect. Organizations with rigid hierarchies or low psychological safety experience stronger pushback.

Practical example: In an AI-driven customer experience program, frontline employees resisted adopting predictive tools. The resistance stemmed from fear of job loss and a lack of clarity about how the tools would augment, rather than replace, their work. Leadership addressed this by providing clear role definitions, demonstrating early wins, and rewarding adoption.

STRAVIB Integration:

- **Responsibility Mapping:** Clarify who does what and when.
- **Integration Maturity:** Ensure cultural readiness is part of the adoption strategy.

Managing Human Side of Change

Challenge	Symptoms	Action	Owner	Timeline
Fatigue	Missed deadlines, low engagement	Sequence initiatives, communicate priorities	Program Lead	90 days
Resistance	Pushback, low adoption	Training, role clarity, incentives	HR / Change Lead	60 days
Culture Misalignment	Conflict, low collaboration	Coaching, workshops, feedback loops	Leadership	Continuous

Aligning Human and Technical Efforts

Successful transformations integrate the human and technical sides. STRAVIB is useful here:

- **Strategy Clarity:** Define desired behaviors and outcomes.
- **Talent Alignment:** Equip teams with the right skills and change champions.
- **Agility in Execution:** Plan incremental adoption cycles to reduce fatigue.
- **Value Realization:** Track adoption metrics alongside technical KPIs.

Callout: Quick Wins for Human Adoption

- Celebrate early adopters publicly.
- Communicate progress consistently to all levels.
- Provide feedback loops and adjust based on team inputs.
- Tie new behaviors to tangible incentives.

Executive Takeaways

1. Human factors are the primary risk to transformation success.
2. Fatigue, resistance, and culture must be measured and managed like any other KPI.
3. Leadership visibility and active sponsorship matter more than technology sophistication.
4. Use STRAVIB to align people, processes, and technology at the same time.
5. Early wins accelerate adoption and reduce skepticism.

Transformation succeeds only when people adopt, adapt, and sustain change. Systems, AI tools, and modernization efforts act as enablers, but the human side is what makes transformation real.

Part II - Strategic Decisions That Make or Break Transformation

Chapter 3 — Build vs Buy: Making the Call Without Slowing the Transformation

Every transformation reaches a fork in the road. Teams debate it for weeks. Boards push for speed. Architects push for control. Vendors pitch one-stop solutions that promise everything under the sun.

Here's the reality. The build versus buy debate is rarely about technology. It's about **strategy, readiness, and risk tolerance.** When it's treated as a purely technical decision, organizations end up overspending, overbuilding, or buying platforms that never fully land.

This chapter removes emotion and politics from the conversation and provides a clear, executive-level way to make the decision.

Why This Decision Is Harder Today

In a modern digital + AI transformation, the stakes are higher because:

- Vendors sell "AI features" before they exist
- Internal teams overestimate their ability to build
- AI talent is scarce
- Integrations are more complex than they look
- Business wants fast ROI and low complexity
- Security and compliance add friction
- Legacy systems limit your options

As a result, leaders often make decisions based on instinct or pressure, rather than through a true transformation lens.

The Three Questions That Clarify Everything

When you're stuck between build and buy, run these three questions first:

1. Does this capability differentiate our business?

If the answer is yes, lean toward **building or customizing.**
If the answer is no, lean toward **buying** and move on.

2. Do we have (or can we acquire) the skills to build and sustain it?

Not just build — **sustain**.
Tech teams often say "yes" emotionally, not realistically.

3. How fast do we need this to land value?

If the clock is ticking, buying accelerates adoption.
If value depends on tight integration or deep control, building pays off over the long term.

These three questions eliminate nearly 70 percent of internal debate.

True Costs People Underestimate

Executives often underestimate:

- The **total cost of ownership (TCO)**
- Ongoing maintenance and security
- Talent churn
- Integration complexity
- Change management
- Data migration effort
- Vendor lock-in risk
- Time-to-value

A vendor demo makes everything look easy because it's scripted.

Internal architects make everything look possible because they're optimistic. Your job as a leader is to ground the conversation in **reality**, not aspiration.

When Build Makes Sense

Build makes sense when the capability is:

- A core differentiator
- Tied directly to customer experience
- Deeply integrated with your proprietary data
- Strategic long-term

- Hard for competitors to copy

Examples:

- Telecom AI models trained on proprietary network data
- Custom workflow engines aligned to unique processes
- Real-time decisioning engines
- Predictive analytics models tailored to your footprint

Build Benefits

- Control
- Customization
- Competitive edge
- Better integration
- No licensing limits

Build Risks

- Long timelines
- Skill gaps
- Higher maintenance cost
- Higher talent dependency

When Buy Is the Smarter Move

Buy when the capability is:

- Commodity
- Non-differentiating
- Best provided by a vendor with economies of scale
- Required quickly
- Hard to build in-house

Examples:

- CRM
- HRIS
- Cloud infrastructure
- ERP
- ITSM platforms
- Collaboration tools

Buy Benefits

- Faster deployment
- Predictable cost
- Vendor support
- Continuous updates
- Lower skill dependency

Buy Risks

- Customization limits
- Integration challenges
- Vendor roadmap control
- Licensing creep

Hybrid: The Modern Reality

The smartest transformations today operate in a **hybrid model**:

- Buy platforms
- Build differentiating layers on top
- Integrate AI models tuned to your data
- Orchestrate everything through APIs
- Keep your IP where it matters

This avoids vendor lock-in and overbuilding. It also aligns perfectly with STRAVIB.

How STRAVIB Guides the Build-vs-Buy Decision

Here's where the framework shines:

S — Strategy Clarity	What's the business outcome? Does this capability differentiate or just operate?
T — Talent Alignment	Do we have the skills to build? Or do we need managed services?
R — Responsibility	Who owns the capability long-term? Who's accountable for adoption?
A — Agility	What's the fastest path to value? Does build slow down the roadmap?
V — Value Realization	How do we measure impact? Which option accelerates value?
I — Integration Maturity	Can we integrate a vendor solution cleanly? Do we need deep customization?
B — Behavioral Adoption	Will teams adopt out-of-the-box workflows? Or do they need custom flows they're used to?

This turns a messy emotional argument into a rational, structured decision.

Build vs Buy Decision Table (STRAVIB-Ready)

Decision Factor	Build	Buy
Differentiation	High	Low
Time-to-Value Required	Slower	Faster
Talent Readiness	Strong internal team	Limited internal team
Long-term Control	High	Medium
Customization Needs	High	Low/Medium
Integration Complexity	High control	Depends on vendor
Cost Curve	High upfront	Predictable subscription
Behavioral Change	Low if you tailor	Higher if you adopt the vendor workflow

Common Traps to Avoid

- Building because "our systems are special."
- Buying because a board member heard about a cool platform
- Underestimating integration cost
- Overestimating internal skill
- Chasing vendor hype
- Forgetting long-term ownership

These traps stall transformations more than any technology barrier.

Executive Takeaways

1. The build versus buy decision is strategic, not technical.
2. Three questions clarify the decision faster than any committee.
3. Hybrid is the modern default, not build or buy, but building and buying smartly.
4. STRAVIB removes bias and turns the debate into a structured outcome.
5. Choose based on differentiation, readiness, speed, and long-term value.

Chapter 4 — Who's to Blame When It Fails?

The Accountability Fog

Most transformations don't fail because of technology. They fail because responsibility gets spread so thin that nobody truly owns anything. Here's the reality. When a transformation derails, everyone suddenly develops amnesia. Leaders blame vendors. Vendors blame unclear requirements. Teams blame leadership. Finance blames the business case. And the truth sits in the middle, untouched, because nobody wants to name it.

This chapter cuts through the politeness and gets to the real accountability traps that sink major transformations, along with what to do about them.

Decisions slow. Risks hide. Issues get escalated into a black hole.

The fog shows up in a few consistent patterns:

Senior leaders sponsor the program but avoid making real decisions

- Vendors steer the roadmap because internal teams defer to them
- Program teams get blamed for delays they cannot control
- Critical integrations fall between groups, with each assuming the other is handling them

When accountability is ambiguous, ownership becomes optional.

Example:

During a global Order management modernization at a telco, four teams believed they "sort of" owned data migration. Three months later, none of them had started. Nobody was incompetent. Nobody was lazy. The ownership model was broken.

The Vendor Echo Chamber

Let's be blunt. Vendors sell optimism. They walk in with polished demos, reference architectures, and ROI curves that look like they were drawn after three cups of espresso.

Executives love this. It creates momentum. It reduces fear. But it also creates two dangerous illusions:

1. **It will work out of the box**
2. **Our organization is more ready than it is**

The echo chamber gets louder when:

- Leadership pushes for quick wins
- Vendors understate integration complexity
- Internal teams stay silent because they fear looking slow or outdated
- The SOW fails to match the glossy pitch

Common outcome:

Vendors promise transformation.

Internal teams deliver workarounds.

Leadership assumes the truth lies somewhere in the middle.

And nobody updates the business case.

The Internal Blind Spots

Executives often believe their organizations are more aligned, more skilled, and more adaptable than they truly are. The gap between expectation and reality is often wide enough to derail an entire program.

A few recurring blind spots include:

- Underestimating technical debt
- Overestimating internal team capacity
- Assuming people will naturally adopt a new operating model
- Delegating transformation leadership to teams without real authority
- Relying on stale data to drive decisions

This isn't about blame. It's about clarity.

Executives don't need perfection. They need truth.

Shared Failure, Distributed Responsibility

The reality is blunt:

Major transformations fail because everyone contributes a small piece of failure — and nobody catches the complete picture early enough.

The solution isn't about finding someone to punish.
It's about building an accountability system that prevents drift.

How STRAVIB Repairs the Gap

Here's how the STRAVIB model prevents the blame game:

1. Strategy Clarity

Everyone knows the purpose. No room for interpretation.

2. Talent Alignment

Roles and ownership are assigned based on capability, not convenience.

3. Responsibility Mapping

This is the chapter hero.
A clear RACI-Plus model eliminates guesswork:

- Who decides?
- Who executes?
- Who signs off?
- Who unblocks issues?
- Who validates outcomes?

If two groups "share" accountability, nobody owns it.

4. Agility in Execution

Every 90 days, teams revisit ownership, remove bottlenecks, and redistribute responsibilities before problems escalate.

5. Value Realization

Ownership extends beyond delivery—someone must own the impact.

6. Integration Maturity

Adoption is assigned to leaders, not implied.
If adoption is "everyone's job," it becomes no one's job.

7. Balance

Leaders stay grounded. Vendors stay honest. Teams stay aligned.

The Anatomy of a Transformation Failure

This simple pattern repeats:

1. **Ambiguous ownership**
2. **Weak governance**
3. **Unrealistic timelines**
4. **Vendor overconfidence**
5. **Leadership under-involvement**
6. **Missed dependencies**
7. **Late-stage firefighting**
8. **Post-mortem that identifies everything except the real cause**

Executives recognize this instantly because they've lived it.

A Simple Fix: The Responsibility Snapshot

A 1-page table that forces clarity before any work begins:

Area	Primary Owner	Decision Maker	Vendor or Role	Risk Owner	Success Metric
Data Migration					
Integration Layer					
AI Use Case Selection					
Cloud Architecture					
Change Management					
Adoption + Training					
Value Tracking					

If this table has more than one owner in any row, the transformation is already in trouble.

The Three Question Filter

Use this anytime a "transformation" idea sounds exciting but you're not sure if it's real or just noise.

```
┌──────────────────────────┐
|   1. SPECIFIC OUTCOME    |
|  What metric, how much,  |
|         by when?         |
└──────────────────────────┘
             |
             |
             ▼
┌──────────────────────────┐
|   2. PROVEN APPROACH     |
|  What evidence shows it  |
| works in our environment?|
└──────────────────────────┘
             |
             |
             ▼
┌──────────────────────────┐
|    3. FAIL-SAFE PLAN     |
|  What if it doesn't work?|
|  Define triggers + backup|
└──────────────────────────┘
```

1. What business metric will improve, by how much, and by when? - If the team can't answer this in one sentence, the idea isn't ready. Real transformation has measurable outcomes, such as revenue, cost, and retention, not vague "strategic impact."

2. What evidence shows this works in an environment like ours? - Proof beats promises. Look for pilots, case studies, or results from similar organizations. If success elsewhere doesn't map to your context, treat it as unproven.

3. What's the plan if it fails? - Define the downside, the kill-switch triggers, and the fallback path. Without a clear exit strategy, you're gambling, not transforming.

An initiative moves to the next box only if the previous one is answered honestly and completely.
If it fails any box, it goes back for refinement or gets dropped.

Executive Takeaways

- Transformations fail because of unclear accountability.
- Vendors don't lie; they sell ambition. Leaders must anchor it to reality.
- Ownership must be explicit, documented, and understood at every level.
- Governance without authority is theater.
- STRAVIB closes the accountability gap by forcing clarity upfront.

Blame doesn't fix anything. Clarity does.
And clarity is the foundation of transformations that actually land.

Part III – Cloud, AI, Modernization in Practice

Chapter 5 — Cloud & AI Transformation Reality

Transformation is everywhere, but reality often falls short of the hype. The C-suite sees "AI-first" strategies, executives talk about cloud migrations, and slides promise cost savings and instant agility. The truth is that most organizations chase the idea of transformation, not the outcomes. Cloud and AI, when implemented poorly, can lead to cost overruns, frustrated teams, and minimal impact. When done right, they fundamentally improve decision-making, agility, and value creation.

This chapter separates myth from reality and provides the tools, metrics, and leadership guidance needed to ensure modern transformations actually land.

Myths & Hype

- Executives frequently assume that deploying new technologies is, by itself, transformational. Common myths include:
- **Cloud automatically reduces costs.** A simple lift-and-shift often increases complexity and costs when a strong governance model is missing. FinOps practices are essential, yet frequently overlooked.
- **AI replaces humans.** The reality is that AI augments decision-making. Without alignment, adoption, and leadership oversight, AI tools often sit idle.

- **Modernization is instant.** Legacy systems, fragmented data, and organizational inertia mean that progress is incremental, not immediate.

Boards often get excited by flashy slides, analysts promise ROI in months, and executives feel compelled to do something. Unfortunately, this approach prioritizes optics over outcomes.

Sidebar: Transformation Myth vs Reality

Myth	Reality
Cloud reduces costs immediately.	Cloud can increase costs without FinOps and governance.
AI replaces humans	AI transforms decisions, not departments.
Modernization = instant greenfield success	Hybrid approaches balance legacy and innovation.

What Actually Transforms

Fundamental transformation happens at the intersection of **decision-making, data readiness, and cultural adoption**.

- **Decision-Making:** AI and cloud technologies reshape processes, workflows, and business decisions. Organizations often underestimate how profoundly these tools change the way leaders make choices.

- **Data Readiness:** Without structured, accurate data, AI models fail, and cloud migrations become expensive. Data is the foundation. Without it, technology delivers little.

- **Cultural Adoption:** People must trust the technology. Leaders must actively sponsor initiatives, clearly communicate benefits, and model the behaviors they expect others to adopt.

Case Vignette:

A global logistics firm moved routing to the cloud and introduced AI, but poor data quality and frequent manual overrides crippled accuracy. After standardizing data and coaching dispatch leaders to trust and appropriately challenge AI recommendations, adoption finally took hold. Delivery accuracy improved, decision-making speed increased fourfold, customer satisfaction rose by 15 percent, and overtime was reduced.

Measuring ROI Beyond Automation

Traditional ROI metrics such as processes automated, hours reduced, and costs removed still matter. But on their own, they tell an incomplete story. The ROI trap appears when organizations apply short-term financial logic to long-horizon transformation work. Metrics designed for equipment purchases or isolated process fixes do not translate cleanly to initiatives that reshape operating models, decision rights, and customer behavior over time.

When leaders rely on those metrics alone, teams are pushed to overpromise near-term gains to justify investments whose real value compounds later. The result is not better accountability. It is distorted expectations, fragile business cases, and erosion of trust when early numbers fail to match the narrative.

The *real* value lies in:

- Faster and better-informed decisions
- Improved forecasting and operational agility
- Reduced escalation and error rates
- New revenue opportunities unlocked through AI insights

Executives should track **outcomes, not outputs**:

Metric Type	Example
Output	% of processes automated
Outcome	Reduction in customer churn
Value	Incremental revenue from predictive analytics

Boards need dashboards that tell the *real story*, not just progress slides.

Data Readiness + Adoption

A data readiness assessment should occur before any AI project planning begins. Leaders need to understand what data exists, where it resides, how accurate it is, and how much effort is required to make it AI-ready. This assessment often reveals that data preparation accounts for roughly 70 percent of the total project effort. Even the most sophisticated algorithms fail without clean data.

Adoption, by contrast, depends on three pillars: **clean data, skilled talent, and cultural trust.**

Checklist for readiness & adoption:

- Structured, high-quality data pipelines
- Clear ownership of data quality and access
- Employee training and engagement programs
- Early adoption champions who model success

Leaders must reinforce adoption consistently. One email, one announcement, or one training session is not enough. Adoption is a behavioral shift that requires visibility, reinforcement, and recognition.

Tool: AI vs Cloud Readiness Scorecard

Dimension	Readiness Score (1–5)	Notes / Actions
Executive Sponsorship		
Talent & Skills		
Data Availability		
Adoption Plan		
Governance & Risk		
ROI Metrics Defined		

This scorecard gives boards and leadership an objective view of organizational readiness, ensuring gaps are identified and addressed before rollout.

Executive Takeaways

1. Most cloud and AI initiatives fail because hype exceeds reality.
2. Transformation happens at the decision, **data, team skill, and adoption levels,** not just through technology deployment.
3. ROI must be measured in outcomes, not outputs.
4. Leaders must sponsor, model, and enforce adoption consistently.
5. Practical frameworks like STRAVIB align initiatives, adoption, and metrics for success.

A framework like STRAVIB ensures initiatives remain aligned, accountable, and measurable at every stage.

Case Study: Success & Failure

- **Success Story:** A large telecom retail store chain implemented AI-driven demand forecasting. They aligned IT, operations, and leadership, structured a clear adoption plan, and established metrics for both output and value. The result: on-shelf availability improved 25%, and revenue increased measurably within 12 months.
- **Failure Story:** A communications enterprise pushed a rapid cloud migration to cut costs, but skipped architecture planning and relied heavily on undertrained teams. Workloads were lifted as-is, driving hosting expenses higher than on-premises. Operational incidents spiked, teams struggled to troubleshoot cloud-native issues, and leadership lost confidence. The program was placed on hold after six months.

Lesson: Success depends less on technology and more on alignment, adoption, and realistic expectations.

Chapter 6 — Legacy Modernization & Business Model Transformation

Most organizations think transformation is about new tools, new platforms, and new systems. The reality is that technology is just the vehicle. True transformation lies in thoughtfully modernizing legacy systems and reimagining business models for the digital and AI era.

This chapter focuses on **how to approach modernization pragmatically and explains why business model reinvention is the ultimate measure of success.**

Incremental vs. Big-Bang Modernization

Legacy modernization often sparks a familiar debate: overhaul everything at once using a big-bang approach, or modernize incrementally. Both approaches involve trade-offs:

- **Big-Bang:** It offers the allure of speed and a fresh start, but it carries high risk. Cost overruns, operational disruption, and employee resistance can derail the initiative.
- **Incremental/Phased:** Lower risk, allows testing, and integrates learnings along the way. Distribute and rotate skilled resources as the phases progress. It demands patience and disciplined sequencing but often delivers sustainable results.

Executive Tip Box — Modernization Approach:

- Big-Bang = Risk & speed
- Incremental = Patience & sustainability
- Decide based on operational tolerance, cultural readiness, and data maturity

Hidden Costs & Technical Debt

Modernization is not just about replacing old systems. Hidden costs often trip executives:

- **Technical Debt:** Years of patchwork fixes, unsupported software, and siloed processes add complexity. Ignoring this complexity increases both risk and cost.
- **Change Fatigue:** Teams are often overloaded with parallel initiatives, which slows adoption.
- **Integration Complexity:** New platforms require additional interfaces, APIs, and governance frameworks.

Key takeaway: Leaders must account for hidden costs upfront and build a realistic modernization budget that includes technical debt remediation.

Business Model Transformation Examples

Business model transformation changes how value is created and captured, not just how existing products and services are delivered. This type of transformation requires rethinking fundamental assumptions about customers, markets, and revenue streams.

The most successful transformations start with market opportunity and work backward to technology requirements. Organizations that begin with technology capabilities and work forward to market applications often build impressive solutions that nobody wants to buy. Technology enables business model transformation, but it does not drive it. True transformation is measured by how the business model evolves:

- **Subscription Models:** SaaS and services shift revenue recognition while enabling recurring income. Subscription models transform one-time purchases into ongoing revenue streams. This shift requires rethinking product development, customer support, and value delivery. Customers pay for sustained value, which means improvements and innovation must be delivered continuously.
- **Platform Ecosystems:** Integrating partners, APIs, and co-innovation efforts enables greater scale and market reach. Platform business models create value by facilitating interactions between different user groups. Successful platforms address the chicken-and-egg problem by attracting both sides of the market at the same time. They

also develop network effects, where each additional user increases the platform's value for everyone.

- **Servitization:** Traditional product companies increasingly offer outcomes instead of units, such as equipment uptime delivered as a service. Servitization transforms product businesses into service-oriented companies by wrapping products with ongoing support, maintenance, and optimization. Instead of selling equipment, organizations sell outcomes. Instead of relying on one-time revenue, they build long-term customer relationships.
- **Lesson:** Transformation without business model alignment is simply operational change, not strategic reinvention.

Sequencing Initiatives

Modernization and business model reinvention must be **sequenced intentionally**:

1. **Stabilize Core Systems:** Ensure foundational technology is reliable.
2. **Introduce Incremental Modernization:** Prioritize high-impact, low-disruption initiatives.
3. **Layer Business Model Changes:** Start with pilot offerings, measure impact, then scale.
4. **Enable Adoption & Integration:** Ensure teams, processes, and data are ready.

Sidebar — Sequencing Executive Tip:

- Prioritize high-value, low-risk initiatives first
- Sequence work by dependency, not desire
- Use small pilots to validate assumptions before scaling

STRAVIB Alignment: Map modernization and business model initiatives against the STRAVIB pillars: strategy clarity, talent alignment, responsibility, agility, value realization, integration maturity, and balance.

Executive Takeaways

Modernization and business model transformation are inseparable. Executives must:

- Treat modernization as an **enabler**, not an end goal.
- Measure success by **impact on customers, revenue, and operational agility**, not just system uptime.
- Sequence initiatives intentionally, balancing risk, adoption, and value.
- Embed governance and metrics early to track both technical and business outcomes.

Story — Platform Transformation Success/Failure

Industry Case Study — Retailer That Modernized in Increments (Success story)

A national apparel retailer spent years struggling with a 20-year-old POS, inventory, and pricing stack. Instead of attempting one massive switch, the company modernized in waves. First came the POS, followed by inventory accuracy tools, and then order orchestration. Each release ran through a 90-day pilot in ten stores before scaling across the full fleet. Within a year, stock accuracy improved from 72 percent to 92 percent, checkout times dropped by 18 percent, and online-to-store order defects were cut in half. Nothing flashy, just consistent wins that compounded over time.

Here's the reality. Modernization began paying for itself long before it was complete. Store managers trusted the rollout because each wave delivered tangible results. Finance saw shrink decline. E-commerce teams saw improved fulfillment. By the time the final component went live, the new system was not a dramatic reveal. It was simply the next logical step. Incremental progress won because the business could absorb change, test reality in controlled phases, and keep cash flowing throughout the transformation.

Industry Case Study — Big-Bang Overreach (Failed Story)

A major retailer attempted to replace its merchandising, supply chain, pricing engine, and store systems in a single, massive cutover. Leadership wanted a single moment where the entire company would level up overnight. What they got instead was data corruption, empty shelves, mismatched pricing, and stores receiving boxes of the wrong items. Inventory accuracy fell below 60 percent, suppliers stopped trusting forecasts, and customer complaints doubled within weeks.

The cost was not only financial, although the project burned through more than 400 million dollars before leadership pulled the plug. The real damage was credibility. Teams stopped believing in transformation. Store managers refused future pilots. IT talent left in frustration. The company spent the next three years undoing the chaos and rebuilding legacy systems it had already declared obsolete. It became a textbook example of how big-bang modernization looks brave on slides but breaks under real-world pressure.

Part IV – Expectations, Execution, and Value

Chapter 7 — Reality vs Expectations

Transformation initiatives often fail not because of technology or strategy alone, but because executive expectations are misaligned with operational reality. Boards are presented with glossy timelines and ambitious KPIs, while teams on the ground confront complexity, cultural resistance, and resource constraints. This disconnect creates friction and fatigue and ultimately leads to delays or failure.

In this chapter, we explore why expectations break down, how misaligned incentives compound the problem, and practical steps leaders can take to bridge the gap.

Executive Expectations vs. Team Reality

Executives often envision transformation as a linear process:

- Clear timelines
- Immediate adoption
- Quick ROI

Teams, however, encounter:

- Legacy system constraints
- Incomplete or messy data
- Competing priorities and resource shortages
- Cultural resistance

The goal isn't to lower ambition. It's to calibrate expectations to what the organization can realistically absorb. Expectations built on optimism will always lose to the constraints embedded in the system.

Misaligned Incentives

In many organizations, transformation fails because incentives encourage the wrong behaviors:

- Executives are rewarded for starting initiatives, not completing them
- Project managers are evaluated on timelines rather than adoption
- Teams are measured on outputs, not outcomes

When incentives reward speed over quality, or appearance over results, the organization delivers exactly that. Alignment across goals, metrics, and rewards is what makes transformations stick.

Executive Insight: Align **goals, metrics, and rewards** across the organization. If incentives are misaligned, even technically sound initiatives fail.

Timeline and Budget Collisions

Another common mismatch arises when **ambitious timelines meet resource realities**:

- Board-approved budgets often underestimate hidden costs such as integration, data cleanup, and change management.

- Project timelines are compressed to appease stakeholders or match market expectations.
- Dependencies between initiatives are overlooked, leading to delays and cost overruns.

Dependencies get overlooked. Hidden work gets ignored. A single missing skill set or a delayed dataset can slow an entire release. When the initial plan isn't grounded in reality, leaders lose credibility trying to hold timelines that never had a chance.

Lesson: Plan with reality in mind. Build buffer into timelines, account for complexity, and measure incremental progress.

Stories from Global Roles

Drawing from global experience, three recurring patterns consistently emerge that executives should note:

1. **Optimism Bias:** Leaders believe initiatives will be faster and cheaper than reality allows.
2. **Shiny-Object Syndrome:** Teams chase new technologies without completing foundational work.
3. **Cultural Disconnect:** Middle managers and frontline staff often feel unheard, leading to disengagement.

These are not market issues. They are human behavior issues. And they will repeat unless leaders actively manage them.

Bridging the Gap: Practical Steps

Expectation Gap Map (Sidebar / Tool)

A one-page tool to align leadership vision with operational reality:

Dimension	Executive Expectation	Ground Reality	Action Needed
Timeline	6 months	12 months	Adjust milestones, communicate rationale
Budget	$5M	$7M	Reallocate resources, track hidden costs
Adoption	100%	60%	Focus on change champions, training, and reinforcement
Metrics	Output-focused	Outcome-focused	Adjust KPIs, reward adoption, and impact

Actionable Steps:

1. **Map reality early:** Use data, team feedback, and pilot programs to set realistic expectations.
2. **Align incentives:** Reward adoption, outcomes, and collaboration across functions.
3. **Communicate clearly:** Ensure the board and executive team understand trade-offs.
4. **Monitor continuously:** Use dashboards and regular reviews to detect misalignment early.
5. **Adjust iteratively:** Don't treat a plan as immutable — course-correct with transparency.

Heatmap – Execution Risk: Risk concentrates predictably across phases. Scores from 1 to 5 indicate where leaders should focus mitigation efforts during short-cycle execution.

How to read this heatmap

Green indicates low execution risk. Yellow signals that progress will slow.

Red indicates the transformation is at risk of delay, cost overruns, or value loss.

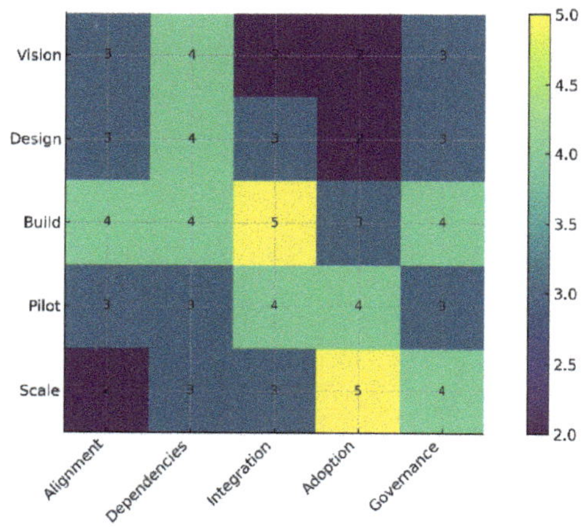

Executive Takeaways

1. Misaligned expectations are the silent killer of transformations.
2. Incentives, metrics, and timelines must reflect operational reality, not just ambition.
3. Leaders must actively bridge gaps with communication, pilots, and feedback loops.
4. Tools like the **Expectation Gap Map** provide clarity and alignment across all stakeholders.
5. Calibrating expectations early is far cheaper than correcting misalignment mid-transformation.

Market Example — Success Story: A Major US Retailer That Reset Its Merchandising With Data

A large national retailer decided to rebuild its merchandising and forecasting capabilities. Instead of chasing a six-month AI overhaul, leadership grounded the plan in operational reality. They understood that legacy systems were inconsistent, store processes varied, and data hygiene was not where it needed to be. As a result, they slowed down upfront, phased delivery, and tightened alignment across teams.

The company invested early in cleaning data pipelines, standardizing store inputs, and, most importantly, adjusting incentives so merchants were rewarded for actually using the new analytics tools. Adoption did not spike overnight, but it climbed steadily from roughly 30 percent in pilot stores to more than 80 percent within eighteen months. Forecast accuracy improved, in-season adjustments became sharper, and inventory accuracy increased across key categories.

The win was not speed. It was clarity and disciplined pacing. Because leaders did not overpromise, the transformation had room to work.

Market Example — Failure Story: A UK Financial Institution's Core System Migration Collapse

A major financial institution attempted a complete core banking migration over a single weekend. Public statements framed it as a seamless switch that customers would not even notice. Internally, teams raised red flags. Data mapping was incomplete, reconciliation rules were unstable, and several integrations remained untested. Despite these warnings, leadership pushed ahead, locked into an ambitious timeline and external commitments.

The cutover failed almost immediately. Millions of customers could not access their accounts. Support teams were effectively blind because their tools were not functioning. Engineers spent days scrambling to fix issues the plan had never realistically accounted for. The recovery effort cost hundreds of millions, triggered regulatory scrutiny, and ultimately led to leadership changes.

The technology did not sink the program. The expectations did.

Chapter 8 — Execution Discipline

Transformation initiatives often fail not because the strategy is wrong, but because execution lacks discipline. Boards see timelines and KPIs, but the real work happens in governance, prioritization, and relentless follow-through. Modern digital and AI transformations demand **structured execution, rapid decision-making, and accountability at every level.**

This chapter provides a playbook for disciplined execution. It outlines what to measure, when to pause, how to kill or push initiatives, and how to run 90-day execution cycles that deliver tangible outcomes.

Governance Without Bureaucracy

Executives frequently default to rigid governance structures, believing that more oversight reduces risk. In reality, excessive bureaucracy slows execution, demotivates teams, and creates paper-only compliance.

Principles for effective governance:

- **Clarity over control:** Define decisions, responsibilities, and escalation paths without micromanagement.
- **Short feedback loops:** Use weekly or bi-weekly checkpoints instead of quarterly reviews.
- **Decision rights architecture:** Assign clear ownership to each element of an initiative.

Executive Tip: Governance should be **enabling, not obstructive**.

Non-Negotiables for Large Programs

Every transformation requires a few non-negotiables to ensure survival:

1. **Executive sponsorship:** Visible, ongoing support from top leadership.
2. **Clear accountability:** No ambiguity on who owns what.
3. **Data-driven decisions:** KPIs and dashboards must be transparent and updated in real time.
4. **Change management:** Adoption strategies are as critical as technical milestones.

Skipping any of these risks failure, regardless of budget or technology.

Metrics That Matter

Traditional transformation metrics often focus on outputs, such as the number of systems deployed, lines of code migrated, or users trained. These measures are necessary but insufficient. **Leaders should also focus on leading and lagging indicators that measure outcomes:**

Metric Type	Example	Insight
Leading	% of users actively using the new platform	Adoption trends
Lagging	Revenue improvement, cost savings	Transformation value

Dashboards should combine both, giving executives a real-time view of where impact is being realized and where corrective action may be required.

Pausing, Killing, or Pushing Initiatives

Execution discipline means making **hard choices**. Not every initiative deserves continued investment.

Decision framework:

1. **Pause:** Temporary obstacles are preventing delivery but can be resolved with minor adjustments.
2. **Kill:** The initiative shows little promise, is misaligned with strategy, or adoption is failing irreversibly.
3. **Push:** Critical initiatives with clear value may require additional resources, stronger sponsorship, or priority rebalancing.

90-Day Execution Cycles

Rather than planning transformations as static, year-long projects, **90-day cycles** enable agility, learning, and continuous course correction.

Cycle steps:

1. **Plan:** Identify key initiatives, owners, and expected outcomes.
2. **Execute:** Focus on high-priority tasks with cross-functional accountability.
3. **Review:** Assess progress, adoption, and value metrics.
4. **Adjust:** Refine priorities, pause low-value items, and scale successful pilots.

Tool — 90-Day Transformation Cycle Template:

Cycle Step	Activities	Owner	Metrics	Notes
Plan	Initiative mapping, resource allocation	PMO	Completion %	Dependencies noted
Execute	Deliverables, adoption tracking	Initiative Owners	Adoption, ROI metrics	Adjust timelines
Review	KPI review, roadblocks identified	Exec Sponsor	Outcome vs output	Course-correct
Adjust	Reprioritize, redistribute resources	Leadership	Alignment, risk mitigation	Scale or kill initiatives

Quick Wins Checklist

Quick wins build momentum and credibility:

- Identify low-risk, high-impact initiatives
- Communicate visible progress early
- Reward early adopters
- Celebrate tangible outcomes to reinforce culture change

Quick wins are **not fluff.** They demonstrate that transformation delivers value and signal seriousness to the organization.

Risk Mitigation in Fast Cycles

Fast cycles move too quickly for traditional, paperwork-heavy risk management. The goal is not to predict every possible problem. It is to spot issues early, respond quickly, and keep momentum intact. When work is organized into ninety-day windows, a one-week delay has greater impact, minor problems compound faster, and assumptions expire sooner. The teams that succeed are not the ones with the thickest risk registers. They are the ones that see trouble coming and adjust before it derails the cycle.

Here's what matters most:

- **Prioritize high-velocity risks** — the ones that can blow up a cycle in days, not months. Think tech failures, missing key people, or late-stage stakeholder pushback.

- **Use rapid, team-based risk scans** — quick, structured sessions that surface real threats instead of theoretical noise.
- **Monitor leading indicators** — early signals like slowed throughput, rising defects, or delayed decisions. If you wait for lagging indicators, you're already behind.
- **Pre-build fast-response playbooks** — clear decision paths and escalation routes so the team isn't improvising under pressure.
- **Accept higher risk tolerance** — fast cycles trade perfect planning for rapid learning. You're aiming for recoverable mistakes, not zero mistakes.
- **Escalate intentionally** — only when something threatens the cycle outcome. Everything else stays with the team.
- **Capture learning immediately** — each cycle teaches you which risks repeat and which can be neutralized earlier next time.

What this really gives you is a way to move quickly without being reckless. You gain speed while also building a buffer against the chaos that usually comes with it. That buffer is what keeps the execution engine stable.

Executive Takeaways

1. Governance should **enable execution**, not create roadblocks.
2. Non-negotiables such as sponsorship, accountability, data, and change management are essential.
3. Measure both leading and lagging indicators to track real outcomes.
4. Make tough decisions by pausing, killing, or pushing initiatives based on value and adoption.
5. Use 90-day cycles to support agility, learning, and sustained progress.
6. Quick wins reinforce momentum and culture, creating a foundation for long-term transformation.

Success: Major Retailer's Data-Driven Merchandising Reset
In the mid-2010s, a large U.S. retailer rebooted its analytics program after early AI efforts underperformed. Rather than attempting a full-scale transformation all at once, leadership broke the work into phased 90-day cycles:

- **Governance Without Bureaucracy:** Decision rights were clarified at both the store and category levels, and weekly standups replaced quarterly reviews.
- **Metrics That Matter:** Both adoption as a leading indicator and revenue per square foot as a lagging indicator were tracked.
- **Quick Wins:** Early improvements in inventory allocation were visible, reinforcing adoption and cultural change. The result was steady adoption, measurable business impact, and scalable transformation without overwhelming teams.
- **Failure: Large Tech Company's AI Health Initiative** A significant technology firm launched an AI-driven oncology health solution, but it struggled to deliver on its promises.
- **Metrics That Matter:** Leading indicators such as clinical adoption and accuracy were weak, yet attention remained focused on the technology rather than on measurable outcomes.

- **Executive Sponsorship:** Initial executive support was strong, but accountability and follow-through at the operational level were inconsistent.
- **Pausing/Killing Initiatives:** Despite clear evidence of adoption issues, programs continued without decisive course correction.
  The result was limited real-world impact, expensive investments, and the eventual scaling back of initiatives.

Lesson: Success comes from disciplined execution, clear metrics, and fast course correction. Failure comes from overpromising, under-measuring, and allowing initiatives to persist despite poor adoption.

Chapter 9 — ROI & Value Realization

Most transformations fail not because the technology is wrong, but because leaders confuse outputs with outcomes. Launching a system, releasing features, or automating processes does not automatically change the business. Boards do not care about deployment metrics. They care about tangible impact. Yet the way many organizations plan transformation almost guarantees poor ROI.

Big-bang programs that span twelve to eighteen months face decaying assumptions, shifting requirements, and technology choices that age before delivery. Early mistakes compound, and a project with a ninety percent monthly success rate can quietly drift into a twenty-four-month slog, burning budget while expected value slips out of reach.

This chapter provides a playbook for realizing value. Define it clearly, track it continuously, and course-correct quickly. Short cycles, visible progress, and honest feedback protect ROI far better than polished Gantt charts ever will.

Defining Value Upfront

Value realization begins long before deployment. Leaders must answer:

- What business problem are we solving?
- How will this initiative improve decisions, revenue, or efficiency?

- What does success look like, both quantitatively and qualitatively?

Executive tip: Articulate expected business outcomes, not just technical deliverables. For example, "launch AI models" is an output, while "reduce inventory shortages by 20 percent" is a value-based outcome. A clear definition upfront sets realistic expectations and aligns teams.

Tracking Outcomes, Not Outputs

Traditional metrics measure what is **produced,** such as the number of systems deployed, features released, or processes automated. Outcomes, by contrast, focus on the **impact those outputs create**. Reporting activity is easy. Systems get deployed. Processes get automated. Features get released. But outputs are meaningless without real effects. The focus must shift to outcomes:

Metric Type	**Example**	**Insight**
Output	Number of AI models deployed	Shows completion but not impact
Outcome	Reduction in inventory shortages	Demonstrates real business value
Value	Increased revenue from predictive insights	Links directly to financial results

Lesson: Dashboards should highlight outcomes over outputs, letting executives see if the transformation actually changes the business.

Leading vs Lagging Indicators

Successful transformations use a mix of leading and lagging indicators:

- **Leading indicators** predict outcomes and enable early course correction, such as adoption rates and process cycle times.
- **Lagging indicators** confirm results, such as revenue growth, cost savings, and customer satisfaction.

This dual view enables rapid learning and keeps transformations on track before minor issues escalate.

Quick Wins Strategy

Quick wins aren't fluff — they create credibility, momentum, and proof of impact.

Steps to identify and execute quick wins:

1. Focus on high-impact, low-complexity initiatives.
2. Communicate results clearly to stakeholders.
3. Use early successes to validate assumptions for larger initiatives.

Quick wins are not just morale boosters. They demonstrate **measurable business impact** and help secure ongoing investment.

Continuous Validation

Value realization is not a one-time exercise. Executives should:

- Use real-time dashboards to track both adoption and business outcomes.
- Adjust investments, priorities, or scope using real-time data.
- Capture lessons from each cycle to refine metrics and processes.

Tool: Value Realization Dashboard

Initiative	Expected Outcome	Current Outcome	Gap	Action
Predictive Forecasting	Reduce stockouts by 20%	15%	-5%	Increase adoption support
AI Chatbot	Improve response time by 30%	28%	-2%	Additional training
Cloud Migration	Reduce cost by 15%	10%	-5%	Review FinOps strategy

Dashboards provide transparency for boards and executives and create a feedback loop for continuous improvement.

Executive Communication

Reporting ROI to boards and stakeholders requires clarity and credibility:

- Focus on **impact, not activity**.
- Use dashboards and stories to illustrate real outcomes.
- Be transparent about gaps, challenges, and corrective actions.

Clear communication builds trust and reinforces that the transformation delivers tangible results.

Executive Takeaways

1. Define value upfront — clarity helps avoid misaligned expectations.
2. Measure outcomes, not outputs, to assess real impact.
3. Use leading and lagging indicators to track and guide transformation.
4. Quick wins validate assumptions and sustain momentum.
5. Continuous validation ensures ROI is realized and gaps are addressed.
6. Communicate results transparently to build trust and credibility.

Market Examples — Success vs. Failure

Success Story — Industrial Manufacturer's Maintenance AI Program

A global industrial manufacturer rolled out an AI-driven predictive maintenance program for its factory equipment.
Here's the key point: they didn't begin with a technology roadmap. They started with the business problem, excessive unplanned downtime.

From day one, they defined clear outcomes:

- cut downtime by 15%
- reduce maintenance labor hours by 10%
- boost throughput in two pilot plants

They built 60–90 day validation cycles using real adoption metrics: technician usage, alert accuracy, and time to intervention. When early pilots showed alerts firing too often, they paused, recalibrated, and improved signal quality. Quick wins, such as preventing a single high-cost compressor failure, built immediate credibility.

By month twelve, downtime had dropped by 18%, and maintenance costs fell by seven figures. Leadership had clear dashboards showing adoption, accuracy, and value. Clear definition upfront plus continuous validation delivered ROI.

Failure Story — National Telecom's Customer Insights Platform

A national telecom launched a large customer insights platform designed to predict churn and identify upsell opportunities. The technology launched on time. The dashboards looked polished. But adoption was dead on arrival.

Why?

No one defined what "value" meant.

Data science teams celebrated models being shipped. Marketing and frontline sales had no clarity on how to use them. The executive team saw only output metrics such as the number of models, number of dashboards, and API uptime. What this really meant was simple: no one tracked whether churn actually declined or whether sales reps used the insights.

Six months later, churn had not moved. Sales leadership stopped asking for updates. The board grew frustrated. The project continued because it appeared active on paper, but no one paused to ask, "Is anyone using this? Is it changing decisions?"

It became a textbook case of output without outcome, and the ROI disappeared.

Part V – Culture, Leadership, and Long-Term Sustainment

Chapter 10 — Human & Cultural Factors

Even the most sophisticated digital or AI transformation will fail if people and culture are not addressed. Systems can be modernized, AI models deployed, and business processes reengineered, but adoption, engagement, and behavior change are what make transformation r**eal and sustainable.**

This chapter explores **why human factors derail** initiatives, how culture influences outcomes, and practical ways to embed change into an organization's DNA.

Transformation Fatigue

Teams often experience **change overload.** Multiple simultaneous initiatives, shifting priorities, and ongoing learning demands can lead to fatigue and burnout.

Symptoms:

- Reduced engagement and productivity
- Resistance to new systems or processes
- Short-term adoption followed by regression

Executive Tip — Managing Fatigue:

- Limit concurrent initiatives per team
- Provide clear priorities and realistic timelines
- Recognize and reward efforts, not just outcomes

Fear & Resistance

Change triggers uncertainty. People fear:

- Job displacement from AI or automation
- New responsibilities without clarity
- Loss of status or influence

Resistance is natural, not a sign of failure. Leaders must **listen, empathize, and communicate purpose**.

Executive Guidance:

- Conduct workshops to surface fears
- Address concerns explicitly in communication
- Show how change aligns with individual and organizational success

Leadership Blind Spots

Even experienced leaders make mistakes in managing human factors:

- Overestimating readiness or skills
- Assuming that communication alone ensures adoption
- Ignoring cultural differences across geographies

Key Takeaway: Leaders must actively **assess readiness and cultural nuances**, not just assume alignment.

Culture Debt

Culture debt is the **accumulation of unaddressed behaviors, norms, and habits** that hinder transformation:

- Informal processes that bypass new systems
- Resistance to new metrics or KPIs
- Lack of cross-functional collaboration

Motivation & Recognition

People adopt change when they see personal and organizational benefits. Motivation strategies include:

- **Visible recognition:** Highlight early adopters and successes publicly
- **Career alignment:** Link transformation skills to promotion or growth
- **Peer influence:** Encourage team-level champions

Embedding Change as Habit

Sustainable transformation requires **habit formation**, not one-time adoption:

- Reinforce new behaviors through repetition and coaching
- Track adoption metrics continuously
- Tie success to individual KPIs and organizational outcomes

Box — Behavioral Nudge Tip:

- Use micro-goals to create early success
- Provide timely feedback
- Celebrate small wins to reinforce behavior

Modern RACI-plus Matrix

Most initiatives fail in the gap between "who does the work" and "who owns the outcome." Traditional RACI does not address decision authority, escalation, or long-term ownership.

RACI-Plus fills that gap by providing:

- Clear decision rights
- Defined escalation paths
- A Success Owner who carries outcomes beyond go-live

If your transformation stalls in meetings or breaks down during handoffs, this framework helps reset the playing field.

The Employee Adoption Psychology in Fast Cycles

Fast cycles stress people more than systems. When change happens quickly, people do not resist the technology; they resist the feeling of losing control or appearing incompetent.

Key truths:

- Speed without safety breaks trust
- Adoption is really a confidence issue
- Micro-wins build belief far better than grand rollouts

When people feel supported and safe, adoption rises naturally.

Executive Takeaways

- **Speed without safety breaks trust.** When change hits people faster than they can process it, resistance isn't sabotage — it's self-protection.
- **Adoption is a confidence problem, not a compliance problem.** If people do not believe they can succeed with the new system, they will avoid it or quietly revert to old ways.
- **Micro-wins beat big announcements.** Visible progress every couple of weeks builds belief in ways no town hall ever will.
- **Symptoms You're Losing the Adoption Battle**
- Employees show "polite compliance" — they nod in meetings but keep using old tools.
- Daily work slows down while people try to blend new processes with old habits.
- Managers act supportive in public but quietly shield their teams from the change.
- You start hearing phrases like "we're not ready yet," "this feels rushed," or "can we wait until next quarter?"
- Training attendance is high, but usage metrics never move.

Success Story — "The Factory Crew Who Took Ownership"

A manufacturing company rolled out a new AI quality inspection system. At first, operators were skeptical. The fear was not about AI; it was about losing judgment and pride.

The turning point came when leadership invited operators to rewrite the inspection criteria alongside the data science team. Suddenly, the system was no longer "AI replacing us." It became "AI powered by us."

Adoption increased rapidly. Defect rates dropped. Operators became internal champions.

When people feel a sense of agency, transformation accelerates.

Failure Story — "The Bank Team That Pretended to Agree"

A bank launched a new workflow platform in a 90-day sprint. There were no complaints and no escalations. Leadership assumed it was a success.

Two weeks later, productivity dropped sharply.

The team had not resisted. They froze. People were afraid of making the wrong click and slowing approvals. Everyone waited for someone "more trained" to take the first step.

Leadership intervened with daily ten-minute confidence check-ins, safe Q&A sessions, and quick micro-demos.

Usage recovered, but only after damage had already occurred.

Silence during change is never a sign of adoption. It is usually fear.

Chapter 11 — Leadership Diploma

Transformation succeeds or fails largely because of **leadership capability.** Technical excellence or strong processes cannot compensate for leaders who fail to inspire, align, or make decisions under uncertainty. Modern digital and AI transformations require leaders with both **strategic clarity and execution discipline,** along with the emotional intelligence to guide teams through disruption.

This chapter introduces the concept of the **Leadership Diploma**, a framework for mastering the skills required to lead successful transformations.

Clarity Under Pressure

Leaders must articulate a clear vision, even in volatile environments:

- Define the transformation objective in simple, actionable terms
- Translate strategy into clear priorities for teams at every level
- Maintain focus despite competing demands and distractions

Executive Tip: Clear messaging reduces ambiguity, builds trust, and increases speed of adoption.

Visible Sponsorship

Sponsorship is not ceremonial. Leaders must **actively participate**:

- Attend key reviews and demonstrations
- Communicate progress and recognize team contributions publicly
- Address obstacles promptly

Communication That Works

Effective leaders communicate **with precision, transparency, and empathy**:

- Avoid jargon; speak in terms that teams understand
- Connect initiatives to employee roles and impact
- Listen actively to concerns, and respond honestly

Building Trust While Changing Rules

Transformation often changes processes, roles, or expectations. Leaders must **maintain credibility**:

- Be consistent in decisions and follow-through
- Acknowledge mistakes and course-correct transparently
- Recognize contributions even when processes change

Decision-Making with Imperfect Data

AI and digital transformations often involve ambiguity. Leaders must:

- Make timely decisions even without complete data
- Define guardrails for acceptable risk
- Iterate and course-correct as insights emerge

Executive Tip: Waiting for perfection delays transformation; timely, informed decisions matter more.

Learning Culture & Balance

Leaders create organizations that **continuously learn**:

- Encourage experimentation and celebrate lessons from failure
- Balance innovation with operational stability
- Embed reflective practices: retrospectives, reviews, and coaching

Tool — Leadership Diploma Checklist

Skill Area	Key Actions	Measurement
Clarity Under Pressure	Define priorities, communicate vision	Team alignment surveys
Visible Sponsorship	Attend reviews, celebrate wins	Adoption metrics, engagement feedback
Communication	Speak in plain language, listen actively	Employee feedback, adoption trends
Trust	Consistency, transparency	Retention, engagement scores
Decision-Making	Timely, risk-aware choices	Speed of execution, ROI
Learning Culture	Reflect, experiment, iterate	Lessons captured, cycle improvements

This checklist serves as a **practical guide for leaders**, ensuring they can execute transformation effectively while nurturing their teams.

Executive Takeaways

1. Leadership capability is the **primary determinant of transformation success**.
2. Clarity, sponsorship, and communication reduce ambiguity and accelerate adoption.
3. Trust and credibility are critical when changing processes or expectations.
4. Decision-making under uncertainty requires courage, discipline, and guardrails.
5. Leaders who embed learning and reflection create sustainable transformation capability.
6. Use the Leadership Diploma checklist as a tool to **self-assess and develop** leadership skills.

Market Example 1 — The Leader Who Showed Up (Success)

A global retailer launched a multi-quarter digital overhaul that was beginning to wobble. Teams were confused, deadlines slipped, and morale declined.

Here's the key point: the turnaround did not come from new software or a new PMO process. It came from the EVP who cleared her calendar and began attending every two-week review. She asked sharp questions, removed blockers on the spot, and publicly recognized teams that made progress.

Within six weeks, priorities were clear. Adoption increased. Teams moved faster because they finally saw the sponsor in the trenches, not just on slides.

Leadership was not a role. It was an action. That single behavior shift stabilized the entire program.

Market Example 2 — The Leadership Vacuum (Failure)

A large financial firm launched an AI-driven underwriting program. On paper, it had everything: funding, talent, and a clean roadmap. But the executive sponsor treated the role as a formality. He delegated every decision, skipped demos, and avoided difficult scope calls.

Teams filled the silence with their own assumptions. Engineering built what it believed the business wanted. Operations waited for guidance on how workflows would change. Marketing did not even know a launch was coming.

By month nine, the system was technically live, but no team trusted it. Adoption stalled, and value evaporated.

The technology was not the failure. The absence of leadership was.

Chapter 12 — Sustaining Transformation

The real challenge in any digital or AI transformation is not launching initiatives. It is **making change stick**. Without intentional sustainment, organizations revert to old habits, new systems underperform, and investments fail to deliver full value.

Sustaining transformation requires a combination of institutionalized behaviors, continuous measurement, governance, and cultural reinforcement. This chapter offers a playbook for embedding change over the long term.

Institutionalizing Behaviors

Change is sustainable when behaviors become habitual:

- Embed new processes into daily routines
- Link responsibilities to roles, KPIs, and performance evaluations
- Encourage repeatable practices across teams

Executive Tip: Repetition, accountability, and incentives drive habit formation.

Continuous Measurement & Feedback

Transformation success is dynamic, so measurement cannot be a one-time exercise:

- Track adoption, efficiency gains, and business outcomes continuously

- Establish dashboards for leaders and teams
- Conduct frequent reviews to identify gaps or drift

Tool: Sustainability Dashboard

Metric	Target	Current	Gap	Action
System Adoption	90%	85%	-5%	Coaching + communication
ROI Realization	$2M	$1.7M	-$0.3M	Adjust scope or process
Process Compliance	95%	88%	-7%	Automation + training

Dashboards make it **easy for executives to spot risk areas** and reinforce progress.

Governance for Sustainment

Governance should continue **beyond launch**:

- Assign owners for ongoing monitoring and enforcement
- Conduct periodic audits to ensure alignment with objectives
- Adjust policies or workflows to accommodate evolving business needs
-

Reinforcing Culture

Culture sustains transformation more than processes or technology:

- Celebrate successes to reinforce desired behaviors
- Encourage peer recognition and knowledge sharing
- Recognize and address cultural debt (resistance, shortcuts, informal workarounds)

Leadership Vigilance

Sustainment requires **active, ongoing leadership attention**:

- Maintain visible sponsorship
- Monitor key metrics, not just KPIs from launch
- Intervene early when adoption or value realization dips

Executive Tip: Leadership vigilance is the glue that keeps transformation from regressing.

The 80/20 Stability Rule

Sustaining transformation requires protecting the core while creating space for controlled innovation. The 80/20 rule provides leaders with a simple operating model:

- **80%** of people, time, and attention stay anchored on the work that keeps the business running.
- **20%** is reserved for structured experiments that shape future capabilities.

What this really means is that innovation should never destabilize the engine that pays for it. Core operations remain steady, predictable, and well supported. Experiments happen in defined "safe zones," where teams can test new ideas without disrupting customers or overloading frontline teams.

When organizations ignore this balance, they burn out teams, stretch resources thin, and introduce chaos into areas that were working well. When they get it right, the organization moves forward without losing stability.

Executive Tip: Protect the core. Innovate in controlled pockets. Scale only what proves it can operate without breaking the business.

Executive Takeaways

1. Transformation is sustained through behaviors, measurement, governance, and culture.
2. Embed new processes into daily routines, roles, and KPIs.
3. Use dashboards and feedback loops for continuous monitoring.
4. Governance must evolve to maintain alignment and performance.
5. Reinforce culture through recognition, peer influence, and celebration of success.
6. Leaders must remain actively involved, as vigilance prevents regression and ensures long-term value.
7. Protect the revenue engine first. Do not experiment where customers feel the impact.
8. Keep innovation contained in "safe zones" so failure does not spill into operations.
9. Slow down before teams burn out or operations become destabilized.
10. Reward both steady operators and innovators equally. Culture weakens when one group feels sidelined.

Success Story — The Manufacturer That Stayed the Course

A global equipment manufacturer rolled out a new digital maintenance system across its plants. The launch went smoothly, but the real win came afterward. Rather than assuming adoption would stick, leadership put sustainment rituals in place: weekly usage reviews, recognition for teams hitting compliance targets, and a simple dashboard showing plant managers exactly where behaviors were slipping.

Here's the key point: those small habits kept teams from drifting back to paper logs. One plant even introduced a peer-coaching rotation that became part of the culture. Twelve months later, process compliance reached ninety-six percent, and unplanned downtime dropped another eleven percent, long after the consultants and project team had moved on.

Why it worked: Governance did not end at launch, and cultural reinforcement turned new behaviors into muscle memory.

Failure Story — The Bank That Slid Back to "The Old Way"

A national bank deployed a workflow automation platform that cut processing time nearly in half during the pilot. Leadership celebrated, declared victory, and moved on. There was no sustainment plan, no behavior tracking, and no clear ownership.

Three months later, teams quietly reverted to their old spreadsheets. Managers did not want to police adoption, training was never refreshed, and workflows were not updated as edge cases emerged. By the sixth month, automation volume had collapsed by more than sixty percent, and the bank lost the efficiency gains it had promoted. The system was technically live but functionally dead.

Why it failed: There was no governance, no cultural reinforcement, and no leadership vigilance. It was a classic slow slide back to comfort.

Part VI — STRAVIB in Action

Chapter 13 — The STRAVIB Framework

The STRAVIB framework serves as the **practical backbone** of transformation, turning strategy into action. While earlier chapters introduced its components, this chapter shows how to apply STRAVIB in real-world initiatives, from planning through execution and review.

The framework emerged from analyzing dozens of transformation initiatives across industries, company sizes, and technology platforms. A clear pattern emerged: initiatives succeeded when the transformation story aligned with organizational reality and failed when it did not. This correlation held regardless of factors such as budget, timeline, or vendor selection.

STRAVIB ensures transformations are **structured, measurable, and sustainable** by aligning leadership, talent, and processes.

STRAVIB Framework Recap

STRAVIB stands for:

- **S**trategy clarity
- **T**alent alignment
- **R**esponsibility mapping
- **A**gility in execution
- **V**alue realization
- **I**ntegration maturity
- **B**alance between innovation and stability

Each component addresses a critical aspect of transformation:

1. **Strategy Clarity:** Identify what truly matters by focusing on high-value initiatives.
2. **Talent Alignment:** Place the right people in roles that match their skills.
3. **Responsibility Mapping:** Clearly define ownership and decision rights.
4. **Agility in Execution:** Plan in 90-day cycles and adapt quickly to change.
5. **Value Realization:** Track outcomes, not just outputs.
6. **Integration Maturity:** Ensure systems and processes work together cohesively.
7. **Balance:** Maintain stability while pursuing innovation.

One-Page STRAVIB Map

A single-page STRAVIB map allows leaders to visualize **initiative alignment** across all seven dimensions:

STRAVIB Component	Initiative	Owner	Status	Priority
Strategy Clarity	AI Claims Forecasting	Head of Ops	Green	High
Talent Alignment	Cloud Migration Team	HR & PMO	Yellow	Medium
Responsibility Mapping	Data Governance	CDO	Green	High
Agility in Execution	90-Day Sprint	PMO	Green	High
Value Realization	Cost Reduction	CFO	Yellow	High
Integration Maturity	ERP Integration	CTO	Red	Medium
Balance	Innovation vs Stability	COO	Green	Medium

This map provides **visibility, accountability, and priority alignment** at a glance.

Mapping Initiatives to STRAVIB

Each transformation initiative should be **evaluated against STRAVIB components**:

- **Assess strategy alignment:** Does the initiative address a critical business problem?
- **Check talent readiness:** Are the right skills and resources assigned?
- **Define responsibilities:** Who decides, executes, and monitors outcomes?
- **Plan agile execution cycles:** Are 90-day checkpoints embedded?
- **Measure value:** How will ROI or outcomes be tracked?
- **Ensure integration:** Are processes and systems connected and functional?
- **Balance stability:** Does innovation create risk, and how is it mitigated?

Story:

A global insurance firm mapped its AI claims initiative to STRAVIB and identified misalignment in talent and gaps in integration. Corrective actions included reassigning specialists and adjusting timelines. Within two cycles, both adoption and ROI improved measurably.

Running 90-Day Cycles

You map out an 18-month transformation with polished milestones and risk plans that look great in a board deck. By month four, shifting user needs, broken technology assumptions, and market changes disrupt the plan. Eighteen months quietly turn into twenty-four. Budgets slip. Benefits stall. Stakeholders tune out. The plan fails because it treats transformation like construction rather than exploration.

A smarter path is ninety-day cycles that deliver something real every quarter. Each cycle produces measurable value, builds momentum, and generates learning to guide the next one. This approach keeps you adaptive without losing direction, because the plan evolves at the pace the business actually moves.

STRAVIB complements **ninety-day execution** cycles by ensuring each initiative is continuously monitored and adjusted:

1. **Plan:** Map initiatives to STRAVIB components.
2. **Execute:** Focus on high-priority tasks with accountability.
3. **Review:** Assess adoption, value, and integration.
4. **Adjust:** Refine priorities, reassign resources, or pivot initiatives.

Tool / Sidebar: 90-Day STRAVIB Cycle Template

Phase	**Activities**	**Owner**	**Metrics**	**Notes**
Plan	STRAVIB mapping, resource allocation	PMO	Alignment %	Dependencies noted
Execute	Deliverables, adoption tracking	Initiative Owners	Adoption, outcome metrics	Adjust timelines
Review	KPI review, integration check	Exec Sponsor	Outcome vs target	Course-correct
Adjust	Reprioritize, redistribute resources	Leadership	Alignment, risk mitigation	Scale or pause initiatives

Governance & Reviews

STRAVIB emphasizes **structured reviews**:

- **Weekly checkpoints:** Operational team alignment and progress
- **Monthly reviews:** Executive oversight and escalation
- **Quarterly audits:** Value realization, integration maturity, and culture adherence

Regular governance ensures that **initiatives remain aligned with strategy and value objectives**.

Quick Wins & Feedback Loops

Even within a disciplined STRAVIB approach, **quick wins build momentum**:

- Identify initiatives that deliver measurable outcomes in short cycles
- Communicate progress clearly across the organization
- Capture lessons learned to refine STRAVIB mapping for future cycles

Templates & Tools

STRAVIB is more than theory; it's a **practical toolkit**:

- **STRAVIB dashboard**: Tracks alignment, adoption, and outcomes
- **Cycle ownership table**: Assigns accountability for each initiative
- **Integration scorecards**: Ensure systems and processes work cohesively
- **Quick wins tracker**: Highlights early successes and lessons learned

These tools ensure STRAVIB is **actionable, repeatable, and measurable**.

Executive Takeaways

1. STRAVIB turns strategy into actionable initiatives with clear accountability.
2. One-page maps create visibility across initiatives, owners, and priorities.
3. Ninety-day cycles enable iterative execution and timely course correction.
4. Governance, reviews, and dashboards maintain alignment and value realization.
5. Quick wins and feedback loops accelerate adoption and build confidence in transformation success.
6. STRAVIB templates enable repeatable and scalable transformation processes for any digital or AI initiative.

Chapter 14 — The Real Transformation

By now, you've seen frameworks, tools, and strategies for digital, AI, and business transformation. But the **true transformation** is not in systems, dashboards, or even STRAVIB alone — it is in **organizational capability and leadership mindset**.

This chapter distills lessons from all prior chapters, showing how to **embed transformation as a capability**, measure lasting impact, and sustain competitive advantage.

Transformation as Capability

Successful organizations treat transformation as a **repeatable capability**, not a one-off project:

- Build processes, frameworks, and governance for ongoing change
- Develop leaders and teams who can manage uncertainty and pivot quickly
- Embed habits that sustain innovation and adoption

Executive Tip: Think of transformation as **muscle memory for your organization** — the more you exercise it, the stronger it becomes.

Embedding STRAVIB

STRAVIB is **not a tool to use once**; it is a living framework:

- Integrate it into strategic planning, budgeting, and project initiation
- Use dashboards and cycle reviews to maintain alignment and accountability
- Continuously update STRAVIB maps to reflect new initiatives, priorities, and risks

Leadership Habits

Transformation-ready organizations are led by executives who practice **repeatable habits**:

- **Regular reflection:** Weekly and quarterly reviews to assess progress and obstacles
- **Visible sponsorship:** Active involvement and celebration of success
- **Decision discipline:** Balancing speed with thoughtful risk management
- **Learning orientation:** Encouraging experimentation and knowledge sharing

Measuring Lasting Impact

Sustainable transformation requires **outcomes-focused measurement**:

- Focus on adoption, value realization, and behavioral change, not just outputs
- Track key leading and lagging indicators
- Monitor both short-term gains and long-term capability development

Tool:

Metric	Target	Measurement	Owner
Adoption Rate	90%	System usage dashboards	PMO
Value Realized	ROI / Outcome metrics	Financial reports	CFO
Behavioral Change	Process adherence	Audit and surveys	COO
Capability Growth	Talent skills & readiness	HR assessments	CHRO

Avoiding Regression

Even after initial success, organizations can **backslide**:

- Leaders must maintain vigilance
- Reinforce new behaviors through incentives, recognition, and coaching

- Update governance and dashboards to reflect evolving business needs

Competitive Advantage & Closing Thoughts

True transformation creates **sustainable competitive advantage**:

- Organizations that embed capability, leadership habits, and culture change are **resilient**
- STRAVIB and related tools provide repeatable success for digital and AI initiatives
- The difference between companies that merely implement and those that lead is **discipline, culture, and human-centric execution**

Executive Takeaways:

1. Treat transformation as a **repeatable capability** embedded in the organization.
2. Apply STRAVIB continuously, not just for one initiative.
3. Cultivate leadership habits that reinforce clarity, trust, and decision discipline.
4. Measure outcomes, adoption, and behavioral change not just outputs.
5. Prevent regression with governance, recognition, and ongoing engagement.
6. The real transformation is **lasting competitive advantage through disciplined execution and human-centric leadership**.

Market Examples — When Transformation Becomes a Capability

Success Story: The Consumer Goods Company That Learned to Pivot

Global consumer goods brand began its AI journey with a few scattered pilots that went nowhere. The breakthrough came when the COO reframed transformation as a capability, not an initiative.

They built a lightweight transformation office, standardized ninety-day cycles, and trained business leaders in decision discipline.

Here's what changed:

- Teams stopped waiting for "perfect data."
- Leaders reviewed adoption and value every cycle.
- STRAVIB-style maps became part of quarterly planning.

Within eighteen months:

- forecast accuracy improved 18%
- three product lines shifted from reactive to predictive planning
- The company cut pilot waste by almost half

The tech didn't suddenly get better.

The organization did.

Cautionary Tale: The Telecom That Forgot to Sustain the Win

A large telecom launched a bold AI-driven customer experience program. Early results looked strong, with faster resolution times, promising pilots, and positive executive attention.

But once the first wave rolled out, leadership moved on to the next shiny initiative.

- No follow-through.
- No habit-building.
- No governance.

Six months later:

- usage dropped nearly 40%
- teams quietly reverted to old manual workflows
- ROI projections collapsed
- dashboards stopped getting updated

The issue was not the technology. It was the absence of repeatable leadership habits and sustained discipline. They had transformation events, not transformation capability, and the gains evaporated.

Appendix / Bonus Tools

The **appendix provides practical, ready-to-use tools and templates** that make STRAVIB and transformation concepts actionable. Leaders can use these tools to support planning, execution, and sustainment.

STRAVIB Templates & Checklists

STRAVIB 1-Page Map Template:

STRAVIB Component	Initiative	Owner	Status	Priority	Notes
Strategy Clarity					
Talent Alignment					
Responsibility Mapping					
Agility in Execution					
Value Realization					
Integration Maturity					
Balance					

STRAVIB Dashboard Template:

Initiative	Owner	Adoption	Value	Status	Next Action
Order-to-Cash Modernization	VP Operations	45%	↓ 22% manual rework	At Risk	Resolve data quality issues before next cycle
Customer Support Transformation	Head of Customer Care	62%	↓ AHT by 18%	On Track	Expand pilot to Tier 2 queues
Supply Chain Optimization	SVP Supply Chain	38%	↑ Forecast accuracy by 12%	Delayed	Align planning cadence with merchandising
Finance Automation	CFO	71%	↓ Close time by 3 days	On Track	Standardize exception rules
Sales Productivity	CRO	29%	↑ Win rate by 6%	At Risk	Rework incentive alignment for reps

IT Cost Optimization	CIO	84%	↓ Run-rate by 15%	Stable	Lock chargeback model for FY

STRAVIB 90-Day Cycle Template:

Phase	Activities	Owner	Metrics	Notes
Plan	Map initiatives, assign resources.			
Execute	Deliverables, adoption tracking			
Review	KPI review, integration check			
Adjust	Reprioritize, redistribute resources.			

Quick Wins Tracker:

Initiative	Expected Outcome	Quick Win Timeline	Actual Result	Key Learnings
Automate Tier-1 Customer Service Inquiries	Reduce agent load by 20% and improve response time	60 days	15% reduction in manual tickets; response time down 22%	Accuracy improved faster than adoption. Training and trust mattered more than model tuning.
Cloud Cost Visibility Dashboard	Establish baseline spend and identify top waste drivers	30 days	92% of workloads tagged; uncovered 18% unused capacity	Visibility changed behavior immediately. Optimization was impossible before this step.
AI-Assisted Order Validation	Increase no-touch order flow by 10%	90 days	No-touch rate increased from 41% to 54%	Data quality, not algorithms, was the limiting factor. Fixing inputs delivered outsized gains.
Predictive Inventory	Reduce stock-out incidents	75 days	Stock-outs down 12%	Store managers trusted alerts

Alerts (Pilot)	in pilot stores		in pilot locations	only after seeing two accurate cycles. Credibility compounds.

Board-Level Build vs Buy Decision Checklist

A one-page decision aid for approving transformation investments

1. Strategic Fit

Does this capability directly support the company's top three strategic priorities?
Does it differentiate us in the market?

If yes → build/customize

If no → buy/accelerate

2. Time-to-Value

How quickly do we need to see measurable impact?
Can a vendor solution deliver the outcome faster?
Is any delay unacceptable because of competitive pressure or operational risk?

3. Talent & Skills Readiness

Do we have the in-house skills to build and sustain this capability?
If not, can we realistically hire or partner to acquire them?
Is long-term ownership feasible?

4. Total Cost of Ownership (TCO)

The board should require BOTH models side-by-side:

Upfront cost

3-year and 5-year run cost

Integration cost

Change management cost

Security & compliance cost

Risk cost (downtime, delays, vendor lock-in)

Red flag: Numbers that only show year-one cost instead of lifecycle cost.

5. Integration Reality

Can the vendor solution integrate cleanly with our data, security model, and legacy stack?

Does building internally create cleaner, more stable integrations?

Are we adding future technical debt either way?

6. Control & Flexibility

Do we need deep customization or IP control?

Will vendor limitations slow us down later?

Will building slow us down now?

7. Risk Profile

Evaluate both options across:

Delivery risk

Talent dependency risk

Vendor dependency risk

Security risk

Scalability risk

Which path carries the least risk *relative to strategic importance*?

8. Value Realization

How will we measure success?

Can we track adoption, impact, and ROI easily?

Does one option accelerate value faster and more reliably?

9. Behavioral Adoption

Will teams adopt vendor workflows as-is?

Or do they require custom flows tied to how they already operate?

What option reduces friction and boosts adoption?

10. Final Decision Check

The board should approve only when the team can clearly

answer:

- Why this option is the fastest **path to value**
- Why it carries lower risk
- Why it supports the **long-term strategy**
- Why alternative paths were **rejected**

Value Realization Dashboard

Metric	Target	Actual	Owner	Action Required
ROI	$X	$Y	CFO	Adjust scope/resources
Adoption Rate	90%	85%	PMO	Coaching/communication
Process Compliance	95%	88%	COO	Automation/training
Capability Growth	Skill level 4	Skill level 3	HR	Training/reallocation

This dashboard ensures **tracking adoption, ROI, and sustainability** at a glance.

90-Day Execution Playbook

1. **Planning:** Map all initiatives to STRAVIB components; assign owners.
2. **Execution:** Focus on top-priority items, monitor adoption and obstacles.
3. **Review:** Evaluate metrics, validate value, and assess integration.
4. **Adjust:** Reallocate resources, adjust timelines, and update STRAVIB maps.

Tip: Integrate lessons learned into the next cycle to create **continuous improvement loops**.

Strategic Fog — How to Spot It and Clear It: A diagnostic tool

Strategic fog emerges when organizations launch more initiatives than their strategy can support. This tool helps leaders spot early warning signs, cut through the noise, and prevent confusion from derailing transformation.

The Strategic Fog Diagnostic

Use these three blunt questions to cut through ambiguity:

1. **What business problem are we solving?**
   If the answer sounds like vendor marketing, pause.
2. **What outcome proves we solved it?**
   If it can't be measured, it won't happen.
3. **What approach gives us the highest chance of success with the capabilities we actually have?**
   Not the aspirational version — the real one.

Most organizations discover that their ambition exceeds their readiness. That clarity is the value.

Clearing the Fog: A Quick Method

- Narrow the initiative list to what actually moves the needle
- Sequence instead of stacking everything in parallel
- Allocate budget based on genuine strategic priority

- Define ownership early and avoid shared accountability
- Measure results, not activities
- Review monthly to catch drift

When to Use This Tool

- Annual planning cycles
- When new "transformations" appear weekly
- Early signs of budget inflation
- Misalignment between what leaders say and what the org funds
- When teams are busy, but value isn't moving

Executive Takeaway

Strategic fog isn't a planning issue. It's a clarity issue.

Clear the fog early, and transformation becomes manageable, measurable, and far more likely to succeed.

The 70-20-10 Talent Strategy for Transformation

Why This Tool Matters

Transformations fail when teams rely too heavily on consultants, hire reactively, or assume internal teams can simply "figure it out."

This tool provides a repeatable framework for building the right mix of people, including **internal talent, strategic hires, and external experts,** without inflating costs or creating long-term dependency.

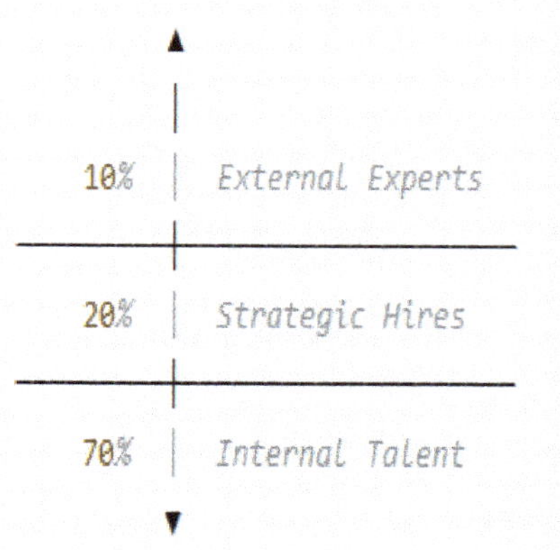

- **70% — Internal Talent (Your Core Engine) -** Develop and empower the people who already understand your business.
- **20% — Strategic Hires (Plug the Critical Gaps) -** Bring in people who provide lasting capability, not just short-term skills.
- **10% — External Experts (High-Precision Specialists) -** Use surgeons, not armies.

When to Shift the Allocation

This isn't dogma — it's a starting point.

- **Strong internal capabilities:** You may drift toward **80-15-5**
- **Weak internal capabilities:** You may start **60-25-15** and grow upward

- The goal is always the same:
  Lower external dependency over time and increase internal ownership.

RACI-Plus: Why It Exists and When to Use It

Transformation Activity	R	A	C	I	D	E	S
1. Requirements & Design							
2. Architecture Decisions							
3. System Build							
4. Testing & QA							
5. Change Management							
6. Go-Live Readiness							
7. Post-Go-Live Support							

What it solves: RACI-Plus cuts through common transformation chaos by clarifying who owns the outcome versus who executes tasks. It breaks endless "waiting for a decision" loops, keeps projects alive after launch through clear long-term ownership, routes escalations to the right people, prevents stakeholders from feeling blindsided, and stops teams from being overloaded with responsibilities they were never meant to carry.

When to Use: Use this tool when you need absolute clarity in transformation planning, when cross-functional work keeps stalling, when decisions slow down or disappear, when success depends on both task completion and long-term adoption, or when the initiative is politically sensitive and getting roles right truly matters.

What It Gives: A clear separation between task execution and outcome ownership, defined decision rights, explicit escalation paths, practical accountability instead of performative checklists, and a shared map teams can use to resolve conflict without pulling senior leaders into every issue.

RACI-Plus Responsibility Categories

Category	What It Really Means	When to Use It
R – Responsible	The people doing the work. They execute tasks, produce deliverables, and coordinate contributors.	Routine tasks, technical work, documentation, testing, training, and configuration.
A – Accountable	The owner of the outcome. Success or failure lands here, regardless of who executed the tasks.	Any activity where results matter beyond task completion (adoption, go-live, performance).
C – Consulted	People who provide input, expertise, and guidance. They influence the work but don't decide.	Technical experts, regulators, SMEs, and impacted business users.
I – Informed	People who need updates after decisions or changes happen.	Status updates, change notifications, schedule shifts, and impact alerts.
D – Decision Authority	The person or group with the power to make binding decisions.	Strategy choices, scope changes, prioritization, and resource allocation.

E – Escalation Path	Where issues go when local decisions hit a wall.	Conflicts, blockers, exceptions, cross-team disputes.
S – Success Owner	The long-term owner after the project ends. They ensure value realization, adoption, and ongoing optimization.	Business outcomes, optimization, operational ownership, and user adoption.

References / Citations

This book draws on a combination of established industry research, academic thought leadership, and real-world transformation experience. Sources include the following categories:

1. **Industry Transformation and Technology Research**
   Insights and data points referenced throughout the book are informed by widely cited industry research from organizations such as **Gartner, McKinsey & Company, and Boston Consulting Group (BCG)**. These sources offer longitudinal analysis on the success rates of digital transformation, cloud economics, AI adoption patterns, and changes to enterprise operating models.

2. **Academic and Practitioner Research on AI, Leadership, and ROI**
   Research and perspectives from **Harvard Business Review** and **MIT Sloan Management Review** underpin discussions on AI adoption, decision-making under uncertainty, leadership behavior, organizational change, and the limitations of traditional ROI models when applied to complex transformations.

3. **Market Examples and Enterprise Case Studies**
   The book references publicly available case studies, industry reporting, and composite market examples drawn from large-scale transformations across **telecommunications, retail, insurance, and global services organizations**, including environments similar to those at

AT&T and other multinational enterprises. Where appropriate, examples have been anonymized or synthesized to focus on patterns and lessons rather than individual organizations.

4. **STRAVIB Methodology and Applied Research** The **STRAVIB framework** presented in this book is based on the author's proprietary synthesis of hands-on leadership experience, applied research, and repeated field application across multiple transformation initiatives. The framework reflects practical patterns observed across strategy execution, talent alignment, accountability, governance, value realization, integration maturity, and the balance between innovation and stability.

Together, these sources form the foundation for a pragmatic, experience-driven view of transformation one that emphasizes execution, leadership behavior, and sustained outcomes over theoretical models or hype-driven narratives

www.ingramcontent.com/pod-product-compliance
Lightning Source LLC
LaVergne TN
LVHW070826220926
848486LV00027B/27